Mr. Food
TEST KITCHEN

WHEEL OF FORTUNE

COLLECTIBLE COOKBOOK

This book could not have come together without the work of many people.
A big thank you goes to everyone on the Mr. Food Test Kitchen team and to the Wheel of Fortune staff and crew.

Mr. Food Test Kitchen: *Chief Food Officer,* Howard Rosenthal; *Test Kitchen Director,* Patty Rosenthal; *Chief Executive Officer,* Steve Ginsburg; *Director of Publishing,* Jodi Flayman; *Test Kitchen Assistants,* Luann Alonso, Dave DiCarlo; *Photographer,* Kelly Rusin; *Photography Assistant,* Jennifer Lett; *Cover Concept & Graphic Elements,* Rachel Johnson; *Director of Business Affairs,* Amy Magro; *Copywriters/Editorial Assistants,* Carol Ginsburg, Yolanda Reid; *Public Relations,* Brenna Fischer; *Website Editors,* Merly Mesa, Brittney Teague; *Business Assistant,* Jaime Gross; *Comptroller,* Roxana DeLima

Book Design, Lorraine Dan of Grand Design
Image Pre-Press Production, Hal Silverman of Hal Silverman Studio

Wheel of Fortune: *Executive Producer,* Harry Friedman; *Vice President of Legal Affairs,* Suzanne Prete; *Producer, Marketing and Promotions,* Lisa Dee; *Senior Marketing and Promotions Manager,* Jessica Wong; *Producer, Publicity and Promotions,* Suzy Rosenberg; *Director of Communications,* Krista Ostensen Osche, *Publicity and Promotions Manager,* Katie Quicksilver Heaney; *Announcer,* Jim Thornton; and the dozens of other Wheel of Fortune staff and crew who have gone above and beyond.
Sony Pictures Entertainment—Consumer Products Publishing Consultant, Virginia King

Pat Sajak and Vanna White, we truly appreciate you graciously allowing us to share the good times that you have brought to the show over the years through your stories, photos, and recipes. Thank you.

"Wheel of Fortune" photo credits to Carol Kaelson, Steve Crise, and Ron Slenzak

Gold seal design on cover: Copyright: <a href='http://www.123rf.com/profile_leonardo255'> / 123RF Stock Photo</a>

Special thanks to Boudin Bakery for providing promotional material for this publication.

The paper used in this printing meets the requirements of the ANSI Standard Z39.48–1992.

To purchase this book for business or promotional use or to purchase more than 50 copies at a discount, or for custom editions, please contact Cogin, Inc. at the address below or info@mrfood.com.

Inquiries should be addressed to:
Cogin, Inc.
1770 NW 64 Street, Suite 500
Fort Lauderdale, FL 33309

ISBN: 978-0-9911934-4-8

Printed in the United States of America
First Edition

www.MrFood.com   www.wheeloffortune.com

We Thank You!

All of us on the Mr. Food Test Kitchen™ team and at Wheel of Fortune® deeply appreciate the time you spend with us on a daily basis. Thank you for inviting us into your home.

We are humbled by all the viewers who have watched and made Wheel of Fortune part of their lives over the years, making it the most successful syndicated TV show of all time. Without you, creating this cookbook would not have been nearly as much fun.

If sharing these recipes and stories with your family
and friends makes your time around the table more fun
and meaningful, then we've accomplished our goal.

Foreword

Growing up in the South, there were two things that were very important and comforting to me, family and food. As a matter of fact, the two always seem to go hand-in-hand because when you live in the South, you can always count on lots of food at family gatherings. And I'm not talking about fancy restaurant dishes. I'm talking about good old-fashioned comfort food.

When I left South Carolina and moved to California, I was afraid that I would miss that loving connection between family and food. After joining Wheel of Fortune, I realized those worries were unfounded. Working at Wheel is like being surrounded by family, and they too share the same passion for family and food that I grew up with.

So when I heard that we were partnering with the Mr. Food Test Kitchen team to create a Wheel of Fortune Collectible Cookbook, I have to tell you, I was super excited. As a matter of fact, the first thing I did was start digging through my personal recipe collection so that I could share some of my favorite family recipes with you. Recipes like my mom's Pineapple Lime Fluff (which was a must have at every family get-together) and my all-time favorite dessert that I call "Vanna Banana Pudding." I got that recipe from my grandmother, along with my passion for crocheting.

As we were working on this book, it was so fun to see how the whole Wheel of Fortune staff and crew came together to share recipes and stories that have been inspired by the show and their families over the years. And the more I thought about it, the more it was evident that food was and still is a huge part of our lives on set and on location. That might be the reason you see categories like "Food and Drink" and "In the Kitchen" so often on the show. And when on location, Pat and I sometimes sneak off to find some good local grub. As a matter of fact, we share some of those dishes in this book as well. Of course, I've even included a few of my kids' favorite recipes. Those are the ones that are "Mom-approved."

I hope with this book you'll build upon the same two loves that I grew up with in the South, as well as here on the show. There is no love better than that of family, which we always celebrate with food. So with these recipes, welcome to our family.

Love,

Vanna White

Do You Remember These Wheel Moments?

Million Dollar Winners

Amazing Puzzle Solves

A Former Contestant Shares His Story

Messy Food Moments

Times To Be Recognized

Memory Lane

Table of Contents

Introduction

For more than 30 years, the Mr. Food Test Kitchen™ team has had a real passion for writing cookbooks, and so do I. I just love creating quick and easy recipes and sharing them with you. For me, it's a way to encourage families and friends to gather around the table. You know what else I've been doing for all these years? Watching Wheel of Fortune! So I thought, "How amazing would it be to combine these two passions?"

I didn't waste any time and reached out to the folks at Wheel of Fortune to share the idea of a *Mr. Food Test Kitchen – Wheel of Fortune Collectible Cookbook*. They loved it! Next thing you know, I'm at their studio in California, with my team, brainstorming how to make an amazing book. While there, I got to watch a bunch of shows being taped, meet Pat and Vanna, and even take a picture with them on the set! And for those of you thinking, "Are they as nice in person as they seem on TV?" The answer is no—they're even nicer!

Of course, everyone knew that Pat and Vanna's favorite recipes had to be in the book, but I also invited the entire Wheel staff and crew to share their best recipes and the stories behind them. Let me tell you, are they ever foodies. Together we also created a Wheel of Fortune Viewer Recipe Contest (see page xiii for more details on that) and all the winning recipes are in here, too.

If you're a Wheel fan, you know that they've taped shows all across the nation, so there are recipes inspired by the local cuisine in the places they've visited—everything from beignets in New Orleans to roast pork in Hawaii. And talk about traveling; no one does that more than the team from the Wheelmobile. So you can count on recipes inspired by places they've been and people they've met with as well.

Don't you wish you could meet some of the contestants who have been on the show and ask them what it was like? Well, this book has the inside scoop from million dollar winners to contestants that have solved puzzles with only one or two letters. They're so talented, you just have to shake your head in amazement!

Beyond making this a cookbook filled with awesome triple-tested recipes, I challenged our whole team to include more. And when I say "more," I mean more behind-the-scenes stories, photos from the show, fun facts, and endless Did You Knows?" It's a one-of-a-kind collection that you won't find anywhere else for those of you who love to cook or just love Wheel of Fortune.

If all that isn't reason enough to cozy up with this book, let me assure you that the recipes for Vanna Banana Pudding and Pat's Perfect Pizza Pie alone are well worth it!

Howard

Howard Rosenthal
On-Air Personality/Chief Food Officer,
21 years at Mr. Food Test Kitchen (and a long time Wheel watcher)

Pat Sajak
Host

Vanna White
Co-Host

Harry Friedman
Executive Producer

Jim Thornton
Announcer

The Mr. Food Test Kitchen™
A Trusted Brand For More Than 30 Years

Over the years, we've seen a lot of food trends come and go and have even gone through a few changes of our own. But through it all, it's been our mission to consistently deliver our triple-tested recipes to millions of home cooks, just like you, through our nationally syndicated TV segments, popular websites, and best-selling cookbooks.

So, what's the secret to our success? Well, our inspiration comes from listening to our viewers and readers while staying true to our founder, Art Ginsburg's, Quick & Easy cooking philosophy. It's a winning combination that serves up plenty of reasons to say ...

"OOH IT'S SO GOOD!!®"

We hope you have as much fun reading and cooking from this book as we had creating it. Oh, by the way, what do you think of our fancy name tags? We think they're "Wheely" fun!

MrFood.com   EverydayDiabeticRecipes.com

The Mr. Food Test Kitchen™ – Wheel of Fortune® Viewer Recipe Contest

There's no better way to pay tribute to all the amazingly loyal Wheel of Fortune and Mr. Food Test Kitchen fans than by giving them a chance to be a part of our history! So we held the first-ever Wheel of Fortune recipe contest, offering viewers an opportunity to share their favorite family recipes and a chance to be included in this collectible cookbook. And boy, did America respond! We received hundreds and hundreds of recipes a day!

After sorting through all the entries, we judged qualifying recipes on creativity, ease of preparation, appearance, and, of course, taste. That meant the Test Kitchen was one busy place! It also meant that there were lots of tastings. Hey, it's a tough job, but someone had to do it! (Thank goodness for stretchy waistbands.)

Thanks to everyone who entered their recipes and shared the stories behind them. There were so many great ones, we could have filled an entire book with them, but, in the end, we had to narrow it down to just 12 winners.

Wanna know who won? Check out the list below or look for the prize-winning ribbon prominently displayed throughout the book.

Congratulations to our Winners!

Contestant for a Day

Have you ever wanted to be a contestant on Wheel of Fortune® or wondered what it would be like to be one? Well, you're not alone! Every year, about a million people apply to be a contestant. Only 10,000 people actually get to audition, and ultimately 600 people are chosen to be on the show. As you can imagine, win or lose, spending the day on the set of Wheel of Fortune is pretty amazing.

Getting Settled In:

On tape days, contestants are picked up from their hotel first thing in the morning and brought to Sony Pictures Studios. Just driving through that iconic gate is exciting! Then they are greeted by the Contestant Department and escorted into the Green Room. When the contestants' guests arrive, (those are the folks who run out on stage when a contestant wins the Bonus Round) they're brought to a special section of the audience in the studio.

The Basics:

As you can imagine, even if you've watched the show for years, there's lots and lots to learn before going on the air. Here, the Contestant Department, Gary O'Brien, Jackie Lamatis, Shannon Bobillo, and Alexandra Reeves, walk contestants through an interactive orientation, so they'll feel confident and comfortable on camera. Consider this like reading the directions before playing a game.

Into the Studio:

At this point, everyone heads to the stage to practice spinning the Wheel, rehearsing their introductions, and calling letters loud and clear. And since Pat and Vanna aren't on the set yet, they have stand-ins who play their roles until it's show time.

Time to Get Ready:

After a catered lunch (who doesn't think better on a full belly?), it's time for makeup, hair, and wardrobe. Between all the bright lights and the high definition cameras, everyone needs to look their best. After all, contestants are seen by more than 13 million viewers a day!

The Luck of the Draw:

Since Wheel tapes six shows in one day, contestants randomly draw a number to determine which show they'll be in. Once the three contestants are selected for each show, their position at the Wheel is determined by a random draw. As they are placed in position, the stage crew adjusts a hydraulic platform under each player, up or down, so that all the contestants look about the same height on TV. Pretty cool, huh?

It's Show Time:

It's the moment everyone's been waiting for! The audience is applauding, the music starts to build, and Jim Thornton, the official announcer of the show, introduces Pat Sajak and Vanna White. At this point, it starts to sink in and the contestants are thinking, "Holy moly, I'm really on Wheel of Fortune!" Then, in no time, Vanna is in position next to the puzzleboard and Pat starts the first Toss-Up Round. It all happens so quickly; it's been called the quickest half hour of a contestant's life.

Just Like You See on TV:

As the show plays out, round after round, it's pretty much like what you see on TV. The main difference is that the contestants have so much more to think about. Where should I look? Should I spin or solve? What letter should I call out? On top of all that, it's hard not to look nervous or starstruck. One thing you don't see at home is that, between rounds, contestants are asked to step away from the Wheel, so the crew can swap out the wedges for the next round.

Everyone is a Winner:

If a player is talented and lucky enough to go to the Bonus Round, they have the chance to win big. And if the contestant wins big ... as in really big, the hardest part is keeping the results secret until the show airs on TV, which is usually several months after taping! Check out some of our favorite stories from contestants on pages 75, 105, 123, 146, 175, and 180.

Want a chance to spin the Wheel and win big? The first step is applying! Check out www.wheeloffortune.com for more details. Good luck!

We've Come a Long Way...

What piece of the Wheel of Fortune® set do you think is most recognized? The puzzleboard or the Wheel? The reality is, they're each a star in their own right. And just as the show has evolved over time so have these two iconic show elements. So, let's take a walk down memory lane.

Some early versions of the set design featured an upright Wheel, much like the type seen at a fair or a carnival.

A New Design:
But ultimately, it was decided to lay the Wheel flat and shoot it with an overhead camera. This not only provided the best view of every spin, but also allowed each contestant to have equal access to the Wheel ... and their own flipper!

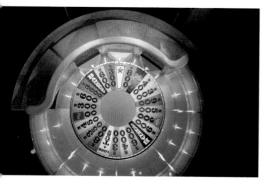

A Real Heavyweight:
Today's Wheel weighs in at more than 2,400 pounds and is constructed on a steel frame surrounded by Plexiglas and more than 200 lighting instruments, which are capable of creating more than 2 million color combinations. To ensure that it spins effortlessly, it rotates on a stainless steel shaft with the help of lots and lots of ball bearings. And, if you are wondering where that telltale clicking sound comes from, here's the secret—it comes from 73 stainless steel pins as they fly over three rubber flippers.

The show's original puzzleboard was made up of 3 rows of 13 triangular prism-shaped objects that turned on a single axle, called "trilons" in the game show industry. Each of the 39 trilons had a green side indicating the space was not being used in a particular puzzle, a blank side which represented that the letter had not yet been revealed, and the side with a letter on it.

The Letter Is:

In the early 1980s, the board was enlarged to four rows, with a total of 52 spaces, and continued to use trilons. Since these boards were operated manually, that meant that each letter had to be physically turned to reveal it. A curtain was dropped in front of the puzzleboard so the crew could change out the letters for the next puzzle.

It's Like Magic:

In early 1997, the puzzleboard was totally updated and became computerized. The new board was made up of 52 touch-activated monitors stacked four high. Rather than having to turn the letters by hand, Vanna could simply touch the right edge of a monitor to magically reveal the letters. It sounds like an easy job, but no one does it better than Vanna.

Try It Yourself:

Ever wished you had Vanna's job? Well, if you get tickets to see a live taping in Culver City, California, make sure you check out the interactive display in the lobby, which allows guests to reveal letters on a sample puzzleboard, just like Vanna. And while you're there, leave yourself a bit of extra time to take in all the memorabilia on the walls before you enter the studio. With more than 30 years of history...it's like walking down memory lane.

Behind the Bonus Round

Ah, the Bonus Round – it's where every contestant wants to end up! Did you know that originally there was no Bonus Round? The contestant who earned the most money was declared the winner. After a few years, to make the show even more exciting, the Bonus Round was introduced. It's changed a bit over time, but winning the Bonus Round is every contestant's dream!

In the Beginning:

Rather than the Bonus Wheel we know today, contestants would select one of five envelopes, each with a prize inside. That envelope was then taken out of rotation for the rest of that week. It was certainly not as glitzy as it is today, but it did the trick. Today's Bonus Wheel, which was introduced in October 2001, has 24 envelopes containing prizes, including cars and cash in different amounts.

Hey, Where Is It?

Have you ever noticed that you never see the Bonus Wheel at the beginning of the show or while the three contestants are playing? That's because it's rolled out and hooked up during the commercial break right before the Bonus Round. Hmmm, now you're thinking about it, aren't you?

Easy Does It:

If you're ever fortunate enough to attend a live taping at Sony Pictures Studios, at the end of the main game, you'll see the stage crew laying out oversized floor mats. This is so the Bonus Wheel can be rolled into position without scratching the high gloss floor. They do this with such precision and coordination; it's almost like watching a ballet.

Now You See It, and Then You Don't:

Then the crew hooks up the electric, secures it to the floor, and polishes it while wearing gloves, until it sparkles. After the Bonus Round, the Bonus Wheel is swiftly rolled off stage in a similar fashion, so it doesn't interfere with the cameras during the closing segment.

So, the next time you're watching the Bonus Round, you'll know about the magic behind it!

So Much to Celebrate!

Over the years, Wheel of Fortune® has celebrated many occasions—everything from special anniversaries to milestone episodes. Grab a cup of coffee or a tall glass of milk as we look back at a few of our favorite tasty and incredibly creative cakes that have been shared (and eaten) on the show. How many of these do you recall?

Did you know that the tradition of a bride and a groom feeding each other cake symbolizes how the couple will feed and nourish their relationship?

In the case with Pat and Vanna, (Host and Co-Host) feeding each other probably symbolizes what a dynamic duo they are on the show.

As for the tradition of smashing cake into each other's faces, no one knows how that started, but with these two, you never know what is next!

The cake to the right, which was created to celebrate the show's 6000th episode, took 5 days to make, and weighed more than 50 pounds!

Do you have a special occasion coming up that is worthy of a wheely outrageous cake? If you do, you may want to try out one of these:

America's Game® ... On Wheels!

If you've never been to a Wheelmobile event, you're missing out! It's the first step in a two-step process to try out to be a contestant on the show. And it's a lot of fun! Applicants are randomly chosen to show off their personalities and their puzzle-solving skills during games led by energetic hosts. The best candidates are invited to a final round of auditions a few weeks after the Wheelmobile event.

Check out Wheelmobile Host, Marty Lublin's story on what it's like traveling with the Wheelmobile, on page 129.

Fun Facts:

- The majority of contestants who appear on Wheel of Fortune were participants at Wheelmobile events.

- Since its inception in 1999, the Wheelmobile has logged more than 350,000 miles and has visited more than 300 cities.

- More than one million Wheel of Fortune fans have attended Wheelmobile events.

Watch for announcements on your Wheel of Fortune station and sign up for Wheel news on www.wheeloffortune.com to find out when the Wheelmobile is coming to your town.

Notes:

Eye-Opening Breakfasts

DECADENT CINNAMON ROLL PANCAKES

Makes 8 pancakes

- 1 stick plus 2 tablespoons butter, divided
- ¾ cup light brown sugar
- 1 tablespoon cinnamon
- 4 ounces cream cheese, softened
- ¾ cup confectioners' sugar
- 1-½ teaspoons vanilla extract, divided
- 2 cups pancake and baking mix
- 1 cup milk
- 2 eggs

1 In a medium microwaveable bowl, melt 1 stick butter. Add brown sugar and cinnamon; mix well. Spoon cinnamon mixture into a quart-size resealable plastic bag and set aside.

2 In a small saucepan over low heat, melt remaining butter; add cream cheese and stir until creamy. Remove from heat and stir in confectioners' sugar and ½ teaspoon vanilla until smooth; set aside.

3 In a large bowl, whisk pancake mix, milk, eggs, and remaining vanilla until well combined. Over medium heat, heat a griddle or large skillet; coat with cooking spray. Pour ¼ cup batter per pancake onto hot griddle. Snip a ¼-inch corner off plastic bag and squeeze cinnamon mixture over each pancake in a swirling pattern. (See below.)

4 Cook 1 to 2 minutes, or until bubbles appear on top of each pancake; flip and cook 1 to 2 more minutes, or until center is set. Remove to a platter, cover, and keep warm. Repeat until all batter is used. Rewarm cream cheese icing, if necessary, and drizzle over pancakes. Serve immediately.

Behind the Recipe:
These decadent pancakes were inspired by the spinning motion of the Wheel, and when they're topped with the ooey-gooey cream cheese icing, it's like winning the Bonus Round of pancakes. Now that's an unbeatable combo!

WESTERN EGG BREAKFAST PIZZA

Makes 8 slices

1 (20-ounce) package refrigerated shredded hash brown potatoes

½ stick butter, melted

½ teaspoon salt

¼ teaspoon black pepper

6 eggs

½ cup diced ham

¼ cup diced onion

¼ cup diced red bell pepper

1 cup shredded Swiss cheese

Sriracha (hot sauce) for drizzling (optional)

1 Preheat oven to 425 degrees F. Coat a 10-inch pizza pan with cooking spray.

2 In a large bowl, combine potatoes, butter, salt, and pepper; mix well. Spread potato mixture evenly over pizza pan and press into a crust shape. Bake 30 minutes.

3 Meanwhile, in a bowl, scramble eggs. Remove crust from oven and spoon eggs over crust. Evenly sprinkle the ham, onion, and red pepper over eggs. Bake 15 minutes, then top with Swiss cheese and bake 5 more minutes, or until cheese is melted. Drizzle with sriracha, if desired, cut into slices, and serve.

Test Kitchen. Mr. Food Hints & Tips

Since this starts with a package of refrigerated shredded potatoes, there's no reason to dig out the box grater, meaning your knuckles will be safe. Once the crust gets crispy, it's ready to top with all sorts of breakfast goodness. And although the recipe is good as is, feel free to mix and match the toppings to make this your very own creation.

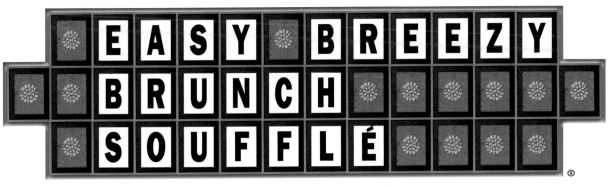

EASY BREEZY BRUNCH SOUFFLÉ

Serves 10

10 eggs

½ cup flour

1 teaspoon baking powder

⅛ teaspoon salt

2 cups small curd cottage cheese

4 cups shredded Monterrey Jack cheese

1 stick butter, melted, then cooled

2 (4-ounce) cans chopped green chilies, drained

1 Preheat oven to 350 degrees F. Coat a 9- x 13-inch baking dish with cooking spray.

2 In a large bowl, whisk together the eggs, flour, baking powder, and salt. Fold in the cottage cheese, Monterrey Jack cheese, and butter. Once mixed, gently add the chilies, then pour into baking dish.

3 Cook 35 to 40 minutes, or until the center has puffed up, it feels firm to the touch, and the edges are slightly browned and crispy.

Behind the Recipe:

"This recipe has been a go-to brunch favorite of mine for years. I've made this for showers and family get-togethers, and it's not uncommon for me to whip up a batch on a Sunday so my family can reheat it for a quick breakfast during the week. Make sure you top each serving with some fresh salsa. Sometimes I even bring some to work to share with the rest of my team. After all, we're like one big family."

Stacy Thapthimthong
Segment Producer
15 years at Wheel of Fortune

GLAZED BACON DONUTS

Makes 10

- 1 cup confectioners' sugar
- 2 tablespoons water
- Vegetable oil for cooking
- 1 (7.5-ounce) package refrigerated biscuits (10 biscuits)
- 2 tablespoons bacon bits

1 In a small bowl, combine confectioners' sugar and water; mix well, then set glaze aside.

2 In a soup pot over high heat, heat 1 inch oil until hot but not smoking. Separate biscuits and lay flat on a cutting board. Using an apple corer or sharp knife, cut out a small circle in center of each biscuit, forming donut shapes.

3 Carefully place the dough in hot oil and cook in batches about 1 minute per side, or until golden. Drain on a paper towel-lined baking sheet. While still hot, dip donuts in glaze, turning to coat completely. Place on a wire rack that has been placed over a baking sheet, to allow excess glaze to drip off. Sprinkle evenly with bacon bits. Serve warm.

Serving Suggestion: If you have a couple of slices of cooked bacon on hand, feel free to crumble them and use them in place of the bacon bits.

If you really prefer chocolate-glazed donuts, add 1 tablespoon unsweetened cocoa to the glaze along with the sugar. Oh, and don't forget to cook up the donut "holes," as those are perfect for snackin'.

Looking Back: If you've been watching the show over the years, you know that Pat and Vanna have enjoyed their fair share of donuts. As you can see, and probably remember, Pat not only likes donuts, but the bigger, the better. He also seems to like it when Vanna shares her stash of donuts with him. Now all she has to do is improve her aim!

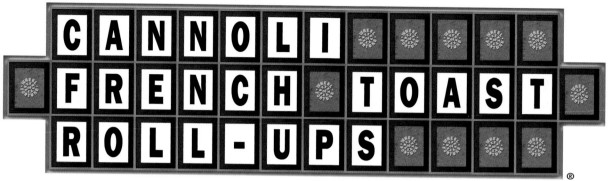

CANNOLI FRENCH TOAST ROLL-UPS

Makes 24 roll-ups

1 (8-ounce) package cream cheese, softened

½ cup ricotta cheese

1 egg yolk

½ cup granulated sugar, divided

¼ cup mini chocolate chips

24 slices white sandwich bread, crusts removed

8 cannoli shells, finely crushed

½ stick butter, melted

Confectioners' sugar for sprinkling

1 In a medium bowl, beat cream cheese, ricotta cheese, egg yolk, and ¼ cup granulated sugar until smooth. Stir in chocolate chips and refrigerate until ready to use.

2 With a rolling pin or a can, roll out each bread slice very thin. Evenly spread cream cheese mixture over each slice of bread. Roll up each slice jelly roll-style and place seam-side down on a baking sheet.

3 In a shallow dish, combine cannoli shells and remaining granulated sugar. Brush butter over roll-ups then roll them in cannoli crumb mixture until completely coated. Return to baking sheet, cover, and freeze at least 2 hours.

4 Just before serving, preheat oven to 400 degrees F and bake roll-ups 10 to 12 minutes, or until golden. Sprinkle with confectioners' sugar and serve immediately.

Test Kitchen. Mr. Food Hints & Tips

The best part of these is that they can be made ahead of time and stored in an airtight container in the freezer. This way all you have to do is pull out as many as you need and bake them off. If you only need a few, your toaster oven will come in real handy.

GRITS WITH HAM & RED-EYE GRAVY

Serves 5

½ stick butter

1 pound sliced ham, cut into ½-inch chunks

½ cup strong brewed coffee

½ cup beef broth

1 tablespoon light brown sugar

¼ teaspoon black pepper

GRITS

3-½ cups water

1 cup white or yellow grits

1 cup shredded sharp Cheddar cheese

½ stick butter

¼ cup milk

½ teaspoon salt

¼ teaspoon black pepper

1 scallion, thinly sliced

1 In a large skillet over medium-high heat, melt ½ stick butter; stir in ham and cook 5 to 7 minutes, or until browned. Remove ham to a plate. Add coffee, broth, brown sugar, and ¼ teaspoon pepper to skillet and cook 3 to 4 minutes, or until bubbly, stirring occasionally.

2 Meanwhile, in a large saucepan over high heat, bring water to a boil. Add grits and cook 5 to 7 minutes, or until mixture is thick, stirring occasionally. Remove from heat and add cheese and butter; stir until melted. Add milk, remaining salt and pepper, and stir until well combined.

3 Spoon grits into a bowl, top with ham and gravy, sprinkle with scallions, and serve immediately.

*Do you ever eat "Brinner"? Oh, if you're wondering what that is, it's when you eat **br**eakfast ... for d**inner**. What a nice change of pace when you feel like having something out of the ordinary while you're watching Wheel of Fortune.*

BAKED EGGS BENEDICT ROLLS®

Serves 4

4 Kaiser rolls

½ cup shredded Muenster cheese

½ cup shredded Cheddar cheese

4 stalks fresh asparagus, trimmed and cut into 1-inch pieces

4 slices Canadian bacon, chopped

6 eggs

¾ cup heavy cream

¼ teaspoon salt

¼ teaspoon black pepper

1 (0.9-ounce) package Hollandaise sauce mix

1 Preheat oven to 375 degrees F. Cut a 2-inch circle off the top of each roll and remove. Hollow out rolls, leaving ½-inch of bread around sides to create a bowl. Place on baking sheet.

2 In a small bowl, combine cheeses; divide mixture evenly into bread bowls. Place equal amounts of asparagus and bacon over cheese.

3 In a medium bowl, whisk eggs, heavy cream, salt, and pepper. Slowly pour egg mixture evenly into rolls. Bake 30 to 35 minutes, or until eggs are set.

4 Meanwhile, prepare Hollandaise sauce according to package directions. Spoon sauce over eggs and serve immediately.

Just think how great this would be to serve as part of a Mother's Day brunch, or on any special occasion. The fun thing about these is, as they bake, the inside gets all ooey-gooey delicious and the outside becomes crispy crunchy. And when you eat them together, you get one incredible treat.

Check out Howard from the Mr. Food Test Kitchen with Pat and Vanna on the set during a recent taping, as the show saluted moms everywhere for all they do.

PEACHES 'N' CREAM DUTCH BABY®

Serves 6

1 stick butter, melted, plus ¾ stick butter, not melted

6 eggs

1 cup milk

½ teaspoon salt

1 cup flour

1 (20-ounce) bag frozen sliced peaches, thawed

¾ cup light brown sugar

1 cup whipped cream

1 Preheat oven to 425 degrees F. Pour the melted butter into a 9- x 13-inch baking dish; set aside.

2 In a blender, combine eggs, milk, and salt; blend until frothy. Slowly add flour, mixing until well blended. Pour into baking dish. Bake 25 to 30 minutes, or until golden brown and center is set.

3 Meanwhile, in a large skillet over medium-low heat, melt remaining butter. Add peaches and brown sugar, and sauté 5 to 7 minutes, or until peaches are tender. Spoon peach mixture over pancake and top with whipped cream. Serve immediately.

Test Kitchen. Mr. Food Hints & Tips

The Test Kitchen used frozen sliced peaches so you can enjoy this all year long, but when fresh peaches are in season, feel free to use them instead. Just make sure you peel 'em first.

JESSICA'S ALL-IN-ONE BREAKFAST®

Serves 1

2 slices whole wheat bread

1 tablespoon butter, softened

2 eggs

½ avocado, peeled, pit removed, and sliced

Salt and pepper to taste

Dash hot sauce (optional)

1 Cut a 2-inch hole in each slice of bread, then evenly butter both sides.

2 In a large skillet over medium heat, toast one side of buttered bread for 2 to 3 minutes, or until golden. Flip over and crack an egg into each hole. Cook until eggs are to desired doneness.

3 Remove to a plate and top with avocado. Sprinkle with salt and pepper and hot sauce, if desired. Serve immediately.

Test Kitchen Tip: If you want sunny-side up eggs, don't flip the bread and egg; for over-easy, cover the skillet for a minute or so. And by flipping them, you get eggs that are medium- to well-cooked, depending on how long you continue to cook them. So, no matter how you like your eggs, these are perfect!

Behind the Recipe:

"I'm an early riser, and I'm not a coffee drinker, so I definitely have to have a hearty breakfast before I start my day at the Wheel of Fortune offices. My favorite thing to make in the morning is what some call 'Eggs in a Basket' with avocado and a splash of hot sauce. I get all the carbs I need from the toast, protein from the egg, and healthy fats from the avocado. It's quick, easy, and best of all, TASTY!"

Jessica Wong
Senior Marketing & Promotions Manager
8 years at Wheel of Fortune

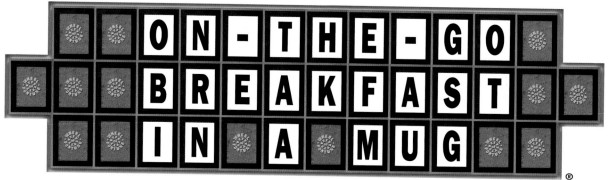

ON-THE-GO BREAKFAST IN A MUG®

Serves 1

2 eggs, beaten

1 tablespoon water

2 teaspoons bacon bits

2 tablespoons shredded sharp Cheddar cheese, divided

1 Coat a 12-ounce microwaveable mug with cooking spray.

2 Add eggs, water, bacon bits, and 1 tablespoon cheese; beat until well blended. Microwave on high 30 seconds; stir.

3 Sprinkle remaining cheese on top and continue to microwave 20 to 30 more seconds, or until egg is set. Serve immediately.

This is perfect when you're short on time, yet still long for a hearty good-for-you breakfast. For students or teachers in a rush, this is the perfect way to make the grade. And, if you're a teacher and want to be a contestant on Wheel, maybe you'll be lucky enough to be chosen for Teachers' Week. Imagine how excited your students would be!

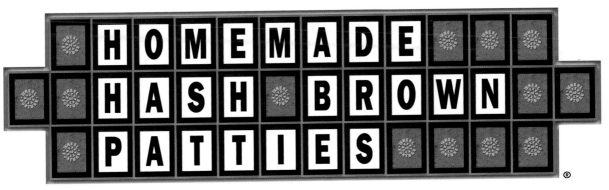

HOMEMADE HASH BROWN PATTIES ®

Makes 12 to 14 patties

- 1 (20-ounce) bag refrigerated shredded potatoes
- ½ cup finely chopped onion
- 1 egg
- ¾ cup flour
- 1 teaspoon salt
- ½ teaspoon black pepper
- 1 cup vegetable oil

1 In a large bowl, combine potatoes, onion, and egg; mix well. Add flour, salt, and pepper; mix until well combined.

2 Measure about ¼ cup potato mixture for each and form into patties.

3 In a large skillet over medium heat, heat oil. Place patties in hot oil and cook 3 to 4 minutes per side, or until golden on both sides. Drain on a paper towel-lined platter. Repeat until all patties are cooked.

Serving Suggestion:

Sure, these are good as they are, but you can personalize them by serving them with a shake or two of hot sauce, ketchup, or even maple syrup. Any way you serve them, you won't be disappointed!

OVERNIGHT PRALINE FRENCH TOAST BAKE ®

Serves 8

1 loaf French bread

10 eggs

3 cups half-and-half

2 tablespoons granulated sugar

1 teaspoon vanilla extract

¾ teaspoon cinnamon, divided

¾ teaspoon nutmeg, divided

2 sticks butter, melted

1 cup light brown sugar

2 tablespoons light corn syrup

1 cup chopped pecans

1 Slice bread into about 20 (1–inch thick) slices. Coat a 9- x 13-inch baking dish with cooking spray. Arrange the bread slices into 2 rows, overlapping slightly. (See photo)

2 In a large bowl, whisk eggs, half-and-half, granulated sugar, vanilla, ¼ teaspoon cinnamon, and ¼ teaspoon nutmeg until well blended. Pour egg mixture over bread, spooning some of the mixture between slices to coat evenly. Cover and refrigerate at least 4 hours or overnight.

3 When ready to bake, preheat oven to 350 degrees F. Meanwhile, combine the melted butter, brown sugar, corn syrup, the remaining ½ teaspoon each of cinnamon and nutmeg, and the pecans; mix well. Sprinkle topping evenly over the casserole.

4 Bake 45-50 minutes or until puffed, golden brown, and the center is set.

Behind the Scenes:

Here, some of the Test Kitchen team reviews the many mouthwatering recipes that were submitted as part of the Viewer Recipe Contest. It was no easy task sorting through stacks and stacks of recipes, testing and tasting them, and then choosing just a handful of winners. It was a tough job, but someone had to do it! Hats off to all of you who entered the recipe contest and shared your family favorites. If only there was more room in this book to add more wonderful entries.

"Several years ago, I went to Las Vegas and, while out for breakfast, I had the most incredible French toast casserole I ever tasted. Loving it so much, I asked if I could get the recipe. Unfortunately, they said it was a house specialty and declined to share it. Bummer. So once I got home, I started experimenting and this is what I came up with. I found it was best when I prepared it the day before, which made this perfect for Christmas morning. What I do is whip up the dry ingredients for the praline topping the night before, after I refrigerate the casserole part. Then, in the morning, I simply sprinkle on the topping, pop it in the oven, set my timer, and let it bake. No big mess. I actually get to spend time with my family instead of spending my time cooking. Best part, everyone really loves it."

Cynthia Adams
Harborcreek, PA

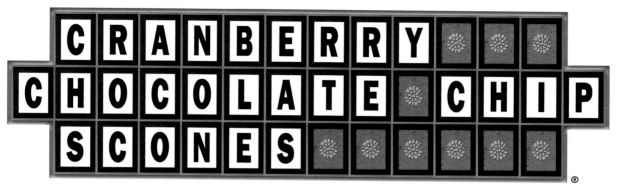

CRANBERRY CHOCOLATE CHIP SCONES

Makes 8 scones

- 1-½ cups plus 1 tablespoon flour, divided
- ½ teaspoon baking soda
- ¼ teaspoon salt
- 2 tablespoons plus ¼ cup sugar, divided
- 1 teaspoon cream of tartar
- 3 tablespoons butter, chilled and cut into pieces
- ¾ cup sweetened dried cranberries
- ½ cup mini chocolate chips
- ¾ cup nonfat buttermilk

1 Preheat oven to 375 degrees F. Coat a baking sheet with cooking spray.

2 In a large bowl, combine 1-½ cups flour, the baking soda, salt, 2 tablespoons sugar, and cream of tartar. Cut in butter with a pastry blender or 2 forks until mixture is coarse crumbs. Add in cranberries and chocolate chips, stirring well. Add buttermilk, stirring just until dry ingredients are moistened.

3 Sprinkle remaining flour evenly over work surface. Place dough onto floured surface; knead 4 or 5 times. Pat dough into a 7-inch circle and place on baking sheet. Score dough into 8 wedges; do not cut through. Sprinkle evenly with remaining sugar.

4 Bake 25 to 30 minutes, or until golden and toothpick inserted in center comes out clean. Let cool, then slice into wedges.

Make it Fun:

How about decorating each wedge with different colored sugar to look like the Wheel? Simply divide the remaining ¼ cup sugar into 4 small bowls, stir in a few drops of food color, and mix until desired color is reached. Then sprinkle each color on wedges right before baking.

LAYERED BLUEBERRY OATMEAL BARS

Makes 21 bars

2-¼ cups old-fashioned oats

2-¼ cups flour

1-½ cups brown sugar

1 cup chopped walnuts

1-½ teaspoons baking soda

½ teaspoon salt

2 sticks butter, melted

3 cups fresh or frozen blueberries

¼ cup granulated sugar

1 tablespoon cornstarch

1 Preheat oven to 350 degrees F. In a large bowl, combine oats, flour, brown sugar, walnuts, baking soda, and salt; pour butter over mixture and mix until crumbly. Press half the oat mixture into a 9- x 13-inch baking dish.

2 In a separate bowl, combine blueberries, granulated sugar, and cornstarch. Mix until blueberries are evenly coated, then distribute evenly over oat mixture in baking dish. Sprinkle remaining oat mixture over blueberries.

3 Bake 25 to 30 minutes, or until golden brown. Cool completely before cutting.

Insider Info:

If you're planning to go visit the Wheelmobile when it comes to town, it might be a good idea to whip up a batch of these the night before and wrap each one in plastic wrap. This way, you'll have something to nibble on during the event. After all, if you get picked to go on stage to try out to be a contestant, you'll need all the energy you can get.

To find out when the Wheelmobile will be in your town, go to www.wheeloffortune.com to sign up for Wheel news and watch for announcements on your local station.

BAKERY-STYLE BONUS ROUND COFFEE CAKE

Serves 10

1 cup chopped pecans

¼ cup light brown sugar

2 tablespoons cinnamon

1 (15.25-ounce) package yellow cake mix

1 cup sour cream

¾ cup vegetable oil

½ cup granulated sugar

4 eggs

1 cup confectioners' sugar

2 tablespoons milk

1 Preheat oven to 350 degrees F. Coat a Bundt pan with cooking spray.

2 In a medium bowl, combine pecans, brown sugar, and cinnamon; mix well. Sprinkle half the nut mixture evenly in Bundt pan.

3 In a large bowl with an electric mixer, beat cake mix, sour cream, oil, granulated sugar, and eggs until smooth. Pour half the batter into the pan, sprinkle with remaining nut mixture, then pour in remaining batter. Bake 40 to 45 minutes, or until toothpick inserted in center comes out clean.

4 Let cool 15 minutes, then invert onto platter to finish cooling. Meanwhile, in a small bowl, whisk confectioners' sugar and milk; drizzle over cake.

Bonus Wheel Fun Facts:

The Bonus Round Wheel holds 24 envelopes. After the 10 seconds that the contestant has to solve the puzzle, whether the puzzle is solved or not, Pat reveals the amount in the envelope. Prizes in this round include cash amounts ranging from $33,000 (commemorating the syndicated version's 33rd anniversary) to a top prize of $100,000, or a vehicle (or two vehicles during weeks with two-player teams). If the contestant enters the Bonus Round with the Million Dollar Wedge, the $100,000 envelope is removed and replaced with a million dollar envelope. Check out the stories of 3 lucky million dollar winners on pages 75, 123, and 146.

BED & BREAKFAST MUFFINS

Makes 12 muffins

- 1-¼ cups plus 2 tablespoons sugar, divided
- 1 stick butter, softened
- 2 eggs
- 2 cups plus 1 tablespoon flour, divided
- 2 teaspoons baking powder
- ½ teaspoon salt
- ½ cup milk
- 1 teaspoon vanilla extract
- 1 tablespoon orange zest
- 1 (12-ounce) package fresh or frozen and thawed cranberries, divided

1 Preheat oven to 375 degrees F. Line a 12-cup muffin tin with paper liners and coat with cooking spray.

2 In a large bowl with an electric mixer on medium speed, beat 1-¼ cups sugar and the butter until creamy. Add eggs one at a time, beating well after each addition. Add 2 cups flour, the baking powder, and salt; beat well. Add milk, vanilla, and orange zest and beat until thoroughly combined. Gently crush ½ cup of the cranberries and stir into batter.

3 In a medium bowl, toss remaining cranberries with remaining flour. Fold into batter and evenly spoon into baking cups. Sprinkle tops with remaining sugar.

4 Bake 25 to 30 minutes, or until a toothpick inserted in center comes out clean. Remove to a wire rack to cool completely.

Behind the Recipe:

This recipe was inspired by all the quaint bed & breakfasts and country inns that have been featured as Wheel of Fortune prizes. Until you win your very own trip, why not make a batch of these and sit back with a cup of coffee? You'll feel like you won a trip to a bed & breakfast. Once you're done pretending, go online and fill out an application to become a contestant. At least you'll be one step closer.

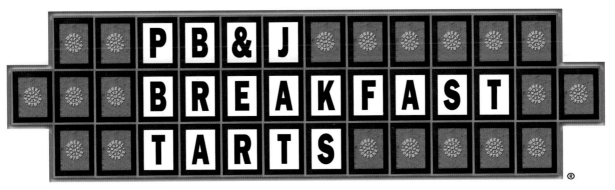

PB&J BREAKFAST TARTS

Makes 12 tarts

1 (14.1-ounce) box rolled refrigerated pie crust

¼ cup peanut butter

¼ cup grape jelly

1 cup confectioners' sugar

1 tablespoon milk

Decorative sugar for garnishing (optional)

1 Preheat oven to 425 degrees F. Coat a baking sheet with cooking spray. Unroll one pie crust and using a knife, trim off the edges to square up. Cut into 12 rectangles, 2 inches wide by 3 inches long.

2 Spread a teaspoon of peanut butter evenly over 6 of the rectangles. Place a teaspoon of jelly in center of peanut butter. Top with remaining rectangles. Using a fork, crimp edges and place on baking sheet. Unroll second pie crust and repeat process.

3 Bake 7 to 9 minutes, or until lightly browned. Let cool 5 minutes, then remove to a wire rack to cool completely.

4 In a small bowl, stir confectioners' sugar and milk until smooth. Spoon glaze slowly over tarts and sprinkle with decorative sugar, if desired. Let harden, then serve.

Make it Homemade:

This homemade version of the popular toaster pastry that so many of you grew up with is not only fun to make, it allows you to create whatever flavor you want. So feel free to mix and match flavors of jellies and jams, maybe try a hazelnut or chocolate spread instead of peanut butter...you get the idea.

RISE & SHINE SMOOTHIES

Serves 2

1 cup fresh strawberries

1 banana

1 ripe mango

¼ cup orange juice

½ cup vanilla yogurt

2 tablespoons honey

1 cup ice cubes

1 Wash and hull the strawberries. Peel the banana and cut it into chunks. Pit, peel, and slice the mango.

2 In a blender, combine all ingredients; blend until smooth. Pour into glasses and serve.

Want to try another flavor combination? Blend up 2 bananas, 2 cups fresh baby spinach, 1 cup ice, ¾ cup vanilla yogurt, 2 tablespoons peanut butter, 2 tablespoons honey, and ⅓ cup milk. Don't let the color throw you…you don't even taste the spinach!!

Behind the Recipe:

On tape days, Kelly Hyatt and the Craft Service team (those are the folks who are responsible for keeping the Wheel of Fortune team fed and happy) have all the fixin's so Pat, Vanna, and the rest of the crew can create their own smoothies backstage. Maybe that's the reason they're always smiling.

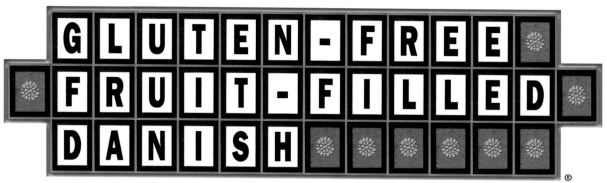

GLUTEN-FREE FRUIT-FILLED DANISH

Makes 14 Danish

- 2 cups gluten-free pancake mix
- ½ stick butter, softened
- 3 tablespoons granulated sugar
- ¾ cup plus 2 tablespoons milk, divided
- ½ teaspoon almond extract
- ⅓ cup fruit preserves or jam, any flavor
- 1 cup confectioners' sugar
- ¼ cup sliced almonds

1 Preheat oven to 400 degrees F. Line two baking sheets with parchment paper.

2 In a large bowl, combine pancake mix, butter, and granulated sugar; mix until crumbly. Stir in ¾ cup milk and the almond extract; mix until combined.

3 Shape into 2-inch balls, and place on baking sheets. Using your thumb, press into center of each ball to make an indentation. Fill each with about a teaspoon of preserves.

4 Bake 13 to 15 minutes, or until light golden around edges. Let cool 5 minutes, then remove to a wire rack to finish cooling.

5 In a small bowl, whisk the confectioners' sugar and remaining milk until smooth. Drizzle over Danish and sprinkle with almonds.

Did You Know?

So often, people expect gluten-free baked goods to lack delicate texture and flavor. That's not the case here! These mini fruit-filled Danish are so moist and tasty, no one would ever know they are gluten-free. The secret is to start with gluten-free pancake mix instead of flour. And, since you can mix and match the fruit preserves, how about using a bunch of different flavors? This way you could serve a platter of these to match all the colors on the Wheel. How's that for a fun idea?

Prize-Winning Appetizers

BUFFALO CHICKEN MAC & CHEESE BALLS

Makes 22 balls

1 (12-ounce) package frozen macaroni and cheese, thawed

½ cup diced cooked chicken

2 tablespoons Buffalo wing sauce

1 egg

1 tablespoon water

1 cup Italian bread crumbs

½ teaspoon garlic powder

¼ teaspoon black pepper

1-½ cups vegetable oil

½ cup blue cheese dressing

1 Line 2 baking sheets with wax paper. In a medium bowl, combine macaroni and cheese, chicken, and wing sauce; mix well. Place in refrigerator 15 minutes to chill. Using a small ice cream scoop, melon baller, or teaspoon, shape mixture into 1-inch balls and place on baking sheets. Freeze 2 hours, or until frozen firm.

2 In a shallow dish, beat egg and water. In another shallow dish, combine bread crumbs, garlic powder, and pepper.

3 In a deep saucepan over medium heat, heat oil until hot, but not smoking. Dip frozen balls into egg wash then roll in bread crumb mixture. In small batches, fry balls 3 to 5 minutes, or until golden brown and center is hot. (Keep remaining balls frozen until ready to fry.) Drain on a paper towel-lined plate and serve immediately with dressing.

Test Kitchen. Mr. Food Hints & Tips

You can fry these in advance and keep them in the fridge or freezer. Patty, who heads up the Mr. Food Test Kitchen and is a big Wheel watcher, shared that if you pop these in your toaster oven when Jim introduces Pat and Vanna, they're toasty hot in plenty of time for the Bonus Round. With that tip, who needs a kitchen timer!

SMOKED TURKEY ROLL-UPS

Makes 48 pieces

- 1 (8-ounce) package cream cheese, softened
- ¼ cup raspberry preserves
- 6 (10-inch) spinach tortillas
- 5 ounces fresh spinach, trimmed
- 1 pound thinly sliced deli smoked turkey
- ¾ cup sweetened dried cranberries
- 12 slices Muenster cheese

1 In a small bowl, combine cream cheese and raspberry preserves; mix well. Lay tortillas out on the counter. Spread mixture evenly over tortillas. Layer with spinach, turkey, cranberries, and sliced cheese.

2 Tightly roll up jelly-roll style and wrap each one in wax paper, twisting ends to seal. Chill at least 2 hours before serving. When ready to serve, unwrap and cut into 1-inch slices.

Serving Suggestion: If you want to make a double batch of the cream cheese-raspberry spread, you can serve the extra as a dipping sauce on the side.

Did You Know?

Ever wondered how big the actual wedges on the Wheel are? They measure about 12" across the top, 5" across the bottom and are about 28" long. And in case you've ever wondered what they're made of, it's compressed layers of laminated card stock or plastic. Specialty wedges, like the $5000 wedge and the Million Dollar wedge, get other vinyls applied on top of the lamination to make them look extra-special.

SECRET INGREDIENT BEAN SALSA

Serves 16

⅓ cup sugar

⅓ cup apple cider vinegar

3 (14.5-ounce) cans diced tomatoes, drained

1 (15-ounce) can black beans, rinsed and drained

1 (15.5-ounce) can corn, drained

1 green bell pepper, chopped

1 onion, finely chopped

4 cloves garlic, minced

⅓ cup loosely packed cilantro leaves

1 In a large bowl, combine sugar and vinegar; mix well. Add remaining ingredients and toss gently until well coated.

2 Cover and chill at least one hour before serving.

Serving Suggestion: Since this is chunkier than your average salsa, try serving it with heartier tortilla chips that can hold up to a big scoop of this veggie-packed dip.

RECIPE CONTEST WINNER

"We were at our neighborhood pool and, at the last minute, it was decided to have a bring-a-snack-to-share party. We went home to see what we could dig up. We had corn chips, but no dip. So we started putting some canned goods together, threw in the green pepper, garlic, and cilantro ... but it lacked flavor. I thought a little sugar might help, so I put that in, but it was still blah. Then a light bulb went off in my husband, Mark's, head, and he added some cider vinegar (his secret ingredient). At that point, we knew we had something. When we brought this back to our neighbors, we got so many compliments. People were trying to guess what the secret ingredient was, but no one could."

Mary Lou Allman
Bloomington, IL

SOUTHERN PICNIC DEVILED EGGS

Makes 12 pieces

- 6 hard-boiled eggs, peeled and cut in half lengthwise
- ½ cup mayonnaise
- 2 teaspoons yellow mustard
- 2 tablespoons sweet relish, drained
- Paprika for sprinkling

1 In a small bowl, mash egg yolks with a fork. Add mayonnaise, mustard, and relish; mix well.

2 Fill egg white halves with yolk mixture and place on a platter. Sprinkle with paprika. Cover with plastic wrap and refrigerate until ready to serve.

Test Kitchen Tip: If you want to learn a few tips and tricks on how to make the perfect hard-boiled eggs, all you have to do is go to mrfood.com and check out the step-by-step how-to video. Just type in "perfect hard-boiled eggs." This way your deviled eggs will be picture perfect.

Did You Know?

Vanna grew up in North Myrtle Beach, South Carolina. So, it's not hard to imagine that she knows a thing or two about Southern cookin'. Although she has lived in California for more than 30 years, she still loves going back home to Myrtle Beach. And you can bet that when she visits, she looks forward to reliving her childhood memories one meal at a time.

SWEET AND TANGY MEATBALLS ®

Makes about 32 meatballs

1-½ pounds ground beef

1 egg

2 tablespoons water

¼ cup dry bread crumbs

1 teaspoon salt

½ teaspoon onion powder

⅛ teaspoon black pepper

1 (12-ounce) jar chili sauce

1 cup grape jelly

2 tablespoons lemon juice

1 teaspoon dry mustard

1 Preheat oven to 350 degrees F.

2 In a large bowl, combine ground beef, egg, water, bread crumbs, salt, onion powder, and pepper; mix well. Form into 1-inch meatballs and place on rimmed baking sheet. Bake 10 minutes.

3 Meanwhile, in a medium saucepan, mix together chili sauce, jelly, lemon juice, and dry mustard. Bring to a boil over medium-high heat, then add meatballs. Reduce heat to low, cover, and simmer 15 to 20 minutes, or until meatballs are cooked through, gently stirring occasionally.

When making meatballs, there are a couple of tips to help make ordinary ones extraordinary. First, don't overmix the meat, 'cause if you do, they'll be chewy. Just mix it until all the ingredients are incorporated. Second, the easiest way to ensure that all the balls are the same size is to use a small ice cream scoop or melon baller to portion the meat before gently rolling it.

DESIGNER HUMMUS DIP

Makes 1-½ cups

1 (15.5-ounce) can chickpeas, drained with ¼ cup liquid reserved

1 tablespoon tahini (ground sesame paste)

2 tablespoons lemon juice

½ teaspoon salt

1 clove garlic, peeled and smashed

1 In a blender or food processor, combine all ingredients; blend until smooth.

2 Place in an airtight container and store in refrigerator until ready to serve.

Serving Suggestion: Make sure you have plenty of cut-up veggies and crackers on hand for dippin'. And drizzle some olive oil for an artistic touch. You can even use this as a healthy sandwich spread since it's good with almost anything.

Behind the Recipe:

"As the Production Designer and head of the Art Department, I'm responsible for designing all the sets or scenic elements for the show ... including the puzzleboard and Wheel. How cool is that! My team and I design these based on the vision of our very talented producers. Let me assure you, we are never bored. At times

we work around the clock. And even though I've worked on the show for more than 30 years, it's still exciting to see the sets come together. Have you noticed there's a new one almost every week? Working on the show has been a fun ride that I hope lasts for many more years."

Renee Hoss-Johnson,
Production Designer
30 years at Wheel of Fortune

Let us introduce to you to the very talented Art Department. It all starts with lots of planning. Above, Shaun Page, Renee Hoss-Johnson, and Jody Vaclav take a break from reviewing drawings on an upcoming set design, while Heather Rasnick looks through the archive wedges to find just the right one.

To the right, Bruce Meisner, Decorator Gang Boss, adds some Polynesian accents to a prop used during an on-location taping in Hawaii. Below, Heather DeCristo (far left) joins the rest of the Art Department staff for a quick picture while in Hawaii. Shaun adds some "life" to one of the sets. The bird looks real, but it's only a prop!

MAGICAL LOADED POTATO PUFFS

Makes 30 puffs

- 1-½ pounds potatoes, peeled and quartered
- 2 tablespoons olive oil
- ½ cup chopped onion
- ½ cup cracker crumbs
- ¼ cup shredded Cheddar cheese
- 2 tablespoons bacon bits
- 2 scallions, thinly sliced
- ½ teaspoon salt
- ¼ teaspoon black pepper
- 2 egg yolks, beaten

1 Preheat oven to 400 degrees F. Coat a baking sheet with cooking spray.

2 Place potatoes in a soup pot and add just enough water to cover them. Bring to a boil over high heat, then reduce heat to medium and cook 15 to 20 minutes, or until fork-tender. Drain off water, mash the potatoes, and allow to cool.

3 In a small saucepan over medium heat, heat olive oil. Add onion and sauté until tender. Add onion, cracker crumbs, cheese, bacon bits, scallions, salt, and pepper to potatoes; mix well. Using your hands, roll mixture into 1-inch balls and place on baking sheet. Brush with egg yolk.

4 Bake 20 to 25 minutes, or until the crust is golden.

Did You Know?

Pat Sajak, who has hosted Wheel of Fortune for more than 30 years, received a star on the Hollywood Walk of Fame in 1994 for his work on the show. But when it was revealed, there was a mistake. They had placed a film camera icon on the star rather than a TV set. No worries, the mistake was quickly corrected. So the next time you're in the Los Angeles area, make sure you stop by and check it out at 6200 Hollywood Boulevard. And after you take a photo there, head a few blocks west and you'll find Vanna's star on the Walk of Fame, too.

CHEESY PEPPERONI PITA WEDGES®

Makes 48 pieces

¾ cup mayonnaise

½ of an 8-ounce package cream cheese, softened

1 cup shredded Cheddar cheese

1 cup shredded mozzarella cheese

½ teaspoon garlic powder

6 (6-inch) pita bread rounds

48 slices pepperoni

1 Preheat oven to 425 degrees F. Coat 2 baking sheets with cooking spray.

2 In a medium bowl, with an electric mixer, beat mayonnaise and cream cheese until smooth. Stir in Cheddar cheese, mozzarella cheese, and garlic powder; mix well.

3 Spread mixture evenly over each pita and top with pepperoni as shown below.

4 Place on baking sheet and bake 7 to 9 minutes, or until topping turns golden. Cut each pita into 8 wedges and serve warm.

Test Kitchen Mr. Food Hints & Tips

These have been tested over and over, and great news: they can be assembled a day or two in advance and simply baked off right before company comes over—or right before Wheel of Fortune comes on. How easy is that? These hold up well because the cream cheese mixture does not make the pita soggy like a traditional pizza sauce would.

ITALIAN ANTIPASTO CUPS

Makes 24 cups

24 slices Genoa salami (see note)

1 cup artichoke hearts, drained and finely chopped

¼ cup finely chopped roasted red peppers

2 tablespoons chopped fresh basil, plus more for garnish

½ cup mini fresh mozzarella balls, cut into quarters

1 (2.25-ounce) can sliced black olives, drained

½ teaspoon Italian seasoning

¼ cup Italian dressing

1 Preheat oven to 400 degrees F.

2 In 2 (12-cup) muffin tins, place one salami slice in each cup. Press salami into cups so it lines the cup. (See photo below.) Bake 6 to 8 minutes, or until salami is crisp. Remove from oven and let cool, then place on serving platter.

3 Meanwhile, in a large bowl, mix artichoke hearts, roasted peppers, basil, mozzarella, olives, Italian seasoning, and Italian dressing. Fill salami cups with artichoke mixture and garnish with extra basil. Serve immediately or chill until ready to serve.

Here, Kelly Rusin, the photographer and an official taster at the Mr. Food Test Kitchen, makes sure that the salami is cut just right, about ⅛-inch thick. If it's too thick or too thin, it won't hold its shape once it's baked. Kelly has a real passion for making everything look picture perfect. Kelly says, "These are so cute and versatile. You could fill them with practically anything from egg salad to potato salad."

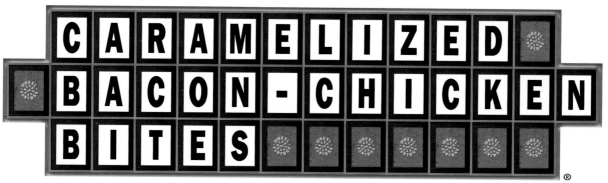

CARAMELIZED BACON-CHICKEN BITES

Makes 36 pieces

½ cup brown sugar

2 tablespoons chili powder

⅛ teaspoon cayenne pepper

18 slices bacon, cut in half

2 boneless, skinless chicken breasts, cut into 1-inch pieces

½ cup honey mustard

1 Preheat oven to 400 degrees F. Line 2 baking sheets with aluminum foil and coat with cooking spray.

2 In a large bowl, combine brown sugar, chili powder, and cayenne pepper; mix well. Wrap a piece of bacon around a piece of chicken. Roll in brown sugar mixture until evenly coated, and secure with a wooden toothpick. Place on baking sheet. Repeat with remaining chicken.

3 Bake 20 to 22 minutes, or until bacon is crispy and chicken is no longer pink. Serve immediately with honey mustard.

Did You Know?
The original name of Wheel of Fortune was Shopper's Bazaar. One major difference between today's syndicated version and the original daytime version was that contestants would win money that they used to buy prizes on the set. My how things have changed!

TWO-MINUTE MEDITERRANEAN TOPPER

Makes about 2 cups

1 cup crumbled feta cheese

¼ cup chopped Kalamata olives

¼ cup finely chopped sundried tomatoes

¼ cup finely chopped red onion

1 tablespoon thinly sliced fresh basil

¼ cup olive oil

2 tablespoons red wine vinegar

1 clove garlic, minced

½ teaspoon dried oregano

¼ teaspoon black pepper

1 In a shallow dish, sprinkle feta cheese in an even layer. Evenly top with olives, sundried tomatoes, red onion, and basil.

2 In a small bowl, whisk remaining ingredients. Pour over feta cheese mixture.

3 Serve immediately or cover and refrigerate until ready to serve.

Serving Suggestion:

This is one of those good-on-everything kind of recipes that only takes a couple of minutes to throw together. Try it on everything from wedges of pita bread and crackers, to salads and pasta. No matter what it's on, with every bite you'll feel like your taste buds won a trip to the Mediterranean—just like many Wheel contestants have over the years.

TEXAS-STYLE SPINACH MELTS

Makes 16 pieces

- 1 (13.5-ounce) box frozen Texas toast garlic bread (8 slices)
- 1 (9-ounce) package frozen creamed spinach
- 1 (14-ounce) can artichokes, drained and chopped
- 3 tablespoons grated Parmesan cheese, divided
- ½ teaspoon onion powder
- 1 cup shredded mozzarella cheese
- Paprika for sprinkling

1 Preheat oven to 400 degrees F. Coat a baking sheet with cooking spray. Place garlic bread on baking sheet and bake 8 to 9 minutes, or until lightly toasted.

2 Meanwhile, heat spinach according to package directions and place in a medium bowl. Stir in artichokes, 2 tablespoons Parmesan cheese, and onion powder. Evenly spoon mixture onto slices of bread. Sprinkle with mozzarella cheese, paprika, and remaining Parmesan cheese.

3 Bake 8 to 10 minutes, or until hot in center and cheese is melted. Cut each slice diagonally in half and serve piping hot.

Behind the Scenes:
We've all heard that everything is BIGGER in Texas, right? Well, that might be true of many things, but when Wheel of Fortune tapes there or at any location, whether it's Hawaii, New York or Chicago, the Wheel is no bigger than the one they use in their studio. Sorry, Texas! That's because there's only one Wheel and one puzzleboard. When the show goes on the road, they get packed up and shipped to each location. But the good news is, these melts are a BIG hit wherever ya serve them.

Can you believe that's the iconic Wheel in the picture below? When the show goes on location the Art Department, lighting directors, and producers work for months designing, plotting and building the sets from the ground up!

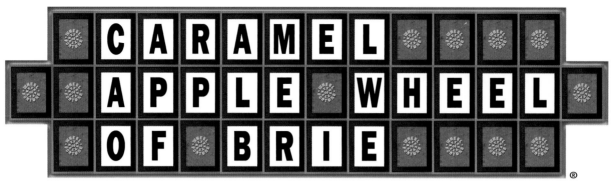

CARAMEL APPLE WHEEL OF BRIE ®

Serves 6

- 1 (8-ounce) can refrigerated crescent rolls
- 1 (8-ounce) round Brie cheese
- 1 egg, beaten
- 2 tablespoons butter
- ½ cup light brown sugar
- ¼ cup heavy cream
- 1 apple, cored, peeled, and coarsely chopped

1 Preheat oven to 350 degrees F. Coat a rimmed baking sheet with cooking spray. Unroll crescent roll dough and pinch seams together. Place Brie in center of dough. Bring dough up over top of Brie, pressing firmly to seal. Place seam-side down on baking sheet and brush with beaten egg. Bake 25 to 30 minutes, or until golden.

2 Meanwhile, in a small saucepan over medium heat, combine butter and brown sugar and cook until sugar dissolves, stirring constantly. Add heavy cream and cook until mixture comes to a boil, stirring constantly. Remove from heat, let cool slightly, then stir in apple.

3 Place Brie on a platter and top with caramel apple mixture. Serve warm.

Did You Know?
Over the years, the price of practically everything has increased, but there's one thing that is no more expensive today than when the show first went on the air. Believe it or not, that is the cost of buying a vowel on Wheel of Fortune. Over all these years, it has never been adjusted for inflation—it's always been only $250. "A bargain!" Pat Sajak says.

Spin-tacular Soups, Salads, & Sandwiches

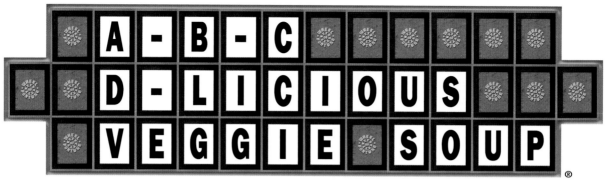

A-B-C D-LICIOUS VEGGIE SOUP®

Serves 6

1 tablespoon vegetable oil

3 carrots, diced

2 celery stalks, diced

1 onion, diced

2 cloves garlic, minced

8 cups chicken broth

4 tablespoons tomato paste

1 teaspoon salt

½ teaspoon black pepper

1-½ cups alphabet-shaped pasta

1 cup frozen peas

1 cup frozen corn

1 In a soup pot over medium heat, heat oil. Add carrots, celery, onion, and garlic and cook 5 minutes, stirring occasionally.

2 Add broth, tomato paste, salt, and pepper and bring to a boil. Reduce heat to low and simmer 20 minutes.

3 Add remaining ingredients and cook another 6 to 8 minutes, or until pasta is tender.

Test Kitchen Tip: If, for some crazy reason, your market doesn't carry alphabet-shaped pasta, feel free to substitute orzo, ditalini or mini shells ... same great taste!

Fun Fact:

Did you know the Executive Producer for Wheel of Fortune, Harry Friedman, is also Executive Producer for JEOPARDY!? Talk about a guy who knows a thing or two about playing games! When asked about this recipe, he said:

"With this soup, all puzzle solutions will be right on the tip of your tongue."

Harry Friedman, Executive Producer 20 years at Wheel of Fortune

POLISH KIELBASA CABBAGE SOUP

Serves 6

- 2 tablespoons vegetable oil
- 5 cups coarsely chopped cabbage
- 1 cup chopped onion
- 3 cloves garlic, minced
- 6 cups chicken broth
- 3 tablespoons white vinegar
- 12 ounces smoked kielbasa, cut into ½-inch slices
- 1 teaspoon salt
- ½ teaspoon black pepper

1 In a soup pot over medium-high heat, heat oil; cook cabbage, onion, and garlic 5 minutes. Add remaining ingredients and bring to a boil.

2 Reduce heat to low and simmer 15 to 20 minutes, or until cabbage is tender.

Serving Suggestion: Why not serve this Polish-inspired soup topped with sliced hard-boiled eggs to give it even more of an Old World taste?

Did You Know?
Over the years, Wheel of Fortune has launched international versions of the show in countries all over the world. Each one has its own personality. If you're ever traveling in a foreign country, and miss watching Wheel of Fortune, check out the TV listings to see if you can find a local adaptation of your favorite game show.

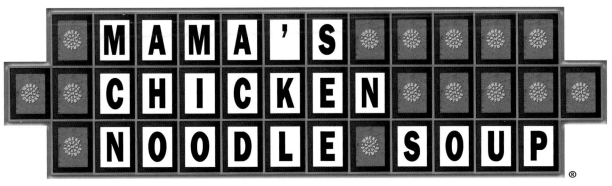

MAMA'S CHICKEN NOODLE SOUP®

Serves 6

1 (2-½- to 3-pound) chicken, cut into 8 pieces

10 cups cold water

3 carrots, cut into chunks

3 parsnips, cut into chunks

2 celery stalks, cut into chunks

1 onion, cut into chunks

1 tablespoon chopped fresh dill

1 tablespoon salt

1-½ teaspoons black pepper

1 (12-ounce) package wide egg noodles

1 In a soup pot over high heat, combine all ingredients except noodles; bring to a boil. Reduce heat to low and simmer 2 to 2-½ hours, or until chicken easily falls off bones.

2 Meanwhile, cook noodles according to package directions.

3 Using tongs, remove chicken to a bowl and allow to cool slightly. Discard skin and bones, and cut up chicken before returning it to soup. Serve in bowls over hot cooked noodles.

Test Kitchen Tip: It's best to refrigerate the soup overnight so that any fat that has risen to the surface can be discarded before reheating

Good For You!

When you're under the weather, nothing is better than curling up on the couch with a bowl of homemade chicken noodle soup while watching Wheel of Fortune. And if you're still on the fence about whether chicken soup, also known as "Jewish Penicillin," is really good for your cold, consider this: studies have shown that a steaming bowl of soup helps loosen congestion. Plus, the fluid helps keep you hydrated.

DINER-STYLE VEGETABLE LENTIL SOUP®

Serves 6

2 tablespoons vegetable oil

1 onion, chopped

3 cloves garlic, minced

½ pound beef top round, cut into ½-inch chunks

3 cups water

5 cups beef broth

1 (12-ounce) package dried lentils, washed and drained

3 carrots, chopped

1 celery stalk, chopped

1 bay leaf

1 teaspoon salt

½ teaspoon black pepper

1 In a soup pot over medium heat, heat oil; sauté onion, garlic, and beef 4 to 6 minutes, or until beef is browned.

2 Add remaining ingredients; bring to a boil over medium-high heat. Reduce heat to low, cover, and simmer 50–60 minutes, or until lentils are tender. Discard bay leaf before serving.

Test Kitchen Tip: To add some extra color to this, why not try using different colored lentils, since they can be found in a rainbow of colors. As for the taste, you can hardly tell the difference, but visually the contrast makes it so much fun.

Behind the Scenes:

As our backstage tour continues, Gary O'Brien, a Producer, chats with contestants before they head into the studio for rehearsal. He's just one of the very talented Contestant Department members that help the contestants feel comfortable before going on-air. Yes, it takes a village to make sure everything goes smoothly once it's showtime.

HEARTY MANHATTAN CLAM CHOWDER®

Serves 6

- 2 tablespoons vegetable oil
- ¼ cup chopped onion
- 2 celery stalks, chopped
- 2 carrots, chopped
- 3 (6-½-ounce) cans chopped clams, not drained
- 1 cup diced potatoes, uncooked
- 1 (28-ounce) can diced tomatoes, not drained
- 1-¾ cups chicken broth
- 1 (8-ounce) bottle clam juice
- ½ teaspoon salt
- ¼ teaspoon black pepper
- ¼ teaspoon dried thyme
- 1 bay leaf

1 In a soup pot over medium heat, heat oil; cook onion, celery, and carrots 5 minutes, or until tender. Add remaining ingredients and bring to a boil, stirring occasionally.

2 Reduce heat to low and simmer 10 to 15 minutes, or until potatoes are tender. Remove bay leaf before serving.

To Fancy It Up: You can pick up a dozen fresh clams, steam them in a skillet just until they open up, and garnish each bowl of soup with them. This way, your guests will think that the entire soup is made with all fresh clams.

Fun Fact:

Wheel of Fortune is broadcast coast to coast. Its biggest TV market is New York City, which is where this classic soup originated. So what do you say you whip up a batch tonight to salute the city that never sleeps?

ITALIAN THREE-BEAN SOUP®

Serves 6

- 1 tablespoon olive oil
- 1 pound Italian sausage, casing removed
- 1 cup chopped onion
- 6 cups chicken broth
- 1 (15-ounce) can great Northern beans, drained
- 1 (15.5-ounce) can pinto beans, drained
- 1 (16-ounce) can chicken peas, drained
- 1 (14.5-ounce) can diced tomatoes
- 2 carrots, cut into ½-inch chunks
- 3 cloves garlic, minced
- ½ teaspoon salt
- ½ teaspoon black pepper
- 3 cups chopped kale

1 In a soup pot over medium-high heat, heat oil; cook sausage and onion 8 to 10 minutes, or until sausage is browned, breaking it up with a spoon.

2 Add remaining ingredients except the kale, and bring to a boil. Reduce heat to low and simmer 30 minutes, or until carrots are tender. Stir in kale and cook 10 more minutes, or until kale is wilted.

Test Kitchen Tip: If your family likes things spicier, feel free to use a spicy Italian sausage, or if you're looking to go a bit healthier, turkey sausage will work just as well.

Behind the Scenes:
You may not know Phil Wayne, Costumer, from watching the show, but he's the one who makes sure that Pat always looks his best. He's also the person who ensures that Pat's ties are perfectly coordinated with whatever Vanna is wearing. Kudos Phil ... Pat always looks marvelous!

NICE & EASY GARDEN GAZPACHO ®

Serves 6

1 (46-ounce) can vegetable juice

1 cup seeded diced cucumber

1 cup diced green bell pepper

1 cup sliced scallions

2 to 3 cloves garlic, finely chopped

6 tablespoons white vinegar

¼ cup olive oil

2 teaspoons salt

2 teaspoons Worcestershire sauce

1 tablespoon hot pepper sauce

1 In a large bowl, combine all ingredients. Cover and refrigerate until chilled.

Serving Suggestion: Top each bowl with a dollop of sour cream right before serving. And feel free to mix and match with any veggies that you have on hand.

Did You Know?

Wheel of Fortune, like this soup, also has ties to gardens. Show segments have been taped in the Hawaii Tropical Botanical Garden on the Big Island, as well as in Madison Square Garden in NYC (ok, that's not really a garden). Talk about getting around all over the country!

MELLOW MUSHROOM SOUP

Serves 5

½ stick butter

1 pound mushrooms, sliced

1 small onion, chopped

½ teaspoon salt

⅛ teaspoon black pepper

5 tablespoons flour

4 cups chicken broth

1 cup half-and-half

¼ teaspoon browning and seasoning sauce

¼ cup sherry (optional)

1 In a soup pot over medium heat, melt butter. Add mushrooms, onion, salt, and pepper; sauté until vegetables are tender.

2 Slowly stir in flour and cook 1 minute, stirring constantly. Stir in broth and bring to a boil, then reduce heat to low and simmer 10 minutes, stirring occasionally.

3 Slowly stir in half-and-half, browning and seasoning sauce, and sherry, if desired. Simmer 5 additional minutes, or until thickened. Serve immediately.

Want to fancy this up? Feel free to use whatever kind of mushrooms you have on hand, whether that's portobello, shiitake, or cremini. You can even mix and match. If you want to keep it simple like we did, we suggest using white button mushrooms.

WEDGED SALAD SKEWERS ®

Makes 8 skewers

8 (1-inch) wedges iceberg lettuce

8 strips cooked bacon (do not over-crisp)

8 grape tomatoes

8 (4-inch) wooden skewers

½ cup blue cheese dressing (see Tip)

1 Thread a wedge of lettuce, a bacon strip, and a tomato onto each skewer. Arrange skewers on a platter, like spokes on a wheel. Place a bowl of the dressing in the middle.

2 Serve immediately, as these are best when the bacon is freshly cooked and not refrigerated.

Test Kitchen Tip: Soak the head of iceberg lettuce in ice cold water for 20 minutes before cutting into wedges. This will ensure that it's nice and crisp. And, to make a wheely good **Homemade Buttermilk Blue Cheese Dressing**, simply whisk together 1 cup mayonnaise, 1 cup buttermilk, ¼ cup crumbled blue cheese, 1 tablespoon minced onion, 1 tablespoon minced fresh parsley, and ¼ teaspoon garlic powder. Chill for one hour before serving.

Fun Fact:
Spinning the Wheel looks a lot easier on TV than it really is. There's a trick to it! Contestants have to lean over the Wheel … really lean over, and give it a good spin. Doing that on a regular basis would be one great workout, but unfortunately contestants are only allowed to appear on the show one time, so don't give up your gym membership just yet!

CASHEW CHICKEN SALAD

Serves 6

4 tablespoons sesame oil, divided

1-½ pounds boneless, skinless chicken breasts, cut into ½-inch chunks

4 cloves garlic, minced

½ cup vegetable oil

⅔ cup sugar

2 tablespoons soy sauce

¼ cup white vinegar

1 head Napa or Chinese cabbage, chopped

¼ pound snow peas, trimmed

½ red bell pepper, cut into ¼-inch strips

½ cup cashew nuts, toasted

1 In a large skillet over medium heat, heat 2 tablespoons sesame oil; sauté chicken and garlic 6 to 8 minutes, or until chicken is no longer pink in center. Remove to a plate.

2 In the same skillet, combine vegetable oil, remaining sesame oil, the sugar, soy sauce, and vinegar; cook 4 to 5 minutes, or until mixture begins to bubble and thicken.

3 Meanwhile, place cabbage, snow peas, bell pepper and chicken in a large bowl or on a platter. Drizzle with dressing and toss until well coated. Top with cashews and serve immediately.

Test Kitchen. Mr. Food Hints & Tips

If you want, you can whip up a batch of the dressing a day or two ahead of time and keep it in the fridge until you're ready to serve it. Pop it in the microwave for a few seconds and you're good to go.

CHUNKY GREEK SALAD WITH FETA

Serves 8

½ cup olive oil

¼ cup red wine vinegar

1 tablespoon lemon juice

3 cloves garlic, minced

1 teaspoon dried oregano

½ teaspoon salt

½ teaspoon black pepper

3 large tomatoes, cut into chunks

2 cucumbers, peeled, cut into chunks

2 green bell peppers, cut into chunks

½ red onion, cut into chunks

½ cup pitted Kalamata olives, drained

½ pound feta cheese, cut into chunks

1 In a medium bowl, whisk olive oil, vinegar, lemon juice, garlic, oregano, salt, and pepper.

2 In a large bowl, combine remaining ingredients. Pour dressing over vegetables and toss until evenly coated. Cover and refrigerate until ready to serve.

Serving Suggestion: If you want to turn this into a main dish, simply top the salad with some cut up grilled chicken or cooked shrimp. And for dessert, don't forget the baklava on page 208.

Did You Know?

If you're ever in Greece, you can tune into their local version of Wheel of Fortune. Just look for the show they call, "O Trochós tis Tíchis." If you can't get to Greece, but still want to take your taste buds on a tasty trip to the Mediterranean, try this salad.

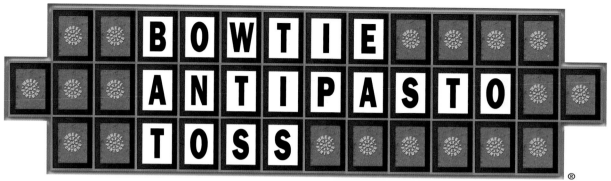

BOWTIE ANTIPASTO TOSS

Serves 10

- 1 (16-ounce) package bow tie pasta
- 8 pepperoncini, drained
- 1 (12-ounce) jar roasted red peppers, drained and sliced
- 1 (14-ounce) can artichoke hearts, drained and quartered
- ½ red onion, cut into ½-inch chunks
- ½ pound provolone cheese, cut into 1-inch chunks
- ½ pound salami, cut into 1-inch chunks
- 1 (16-ounce) can black olives, drained
- ¾ cup Italian dressing

1 In a large pot of boiling salted water, cook pasta according to package directions; drain, rinse, drain again, and cool slightly.

2 In a large bowl, combine remaining ingredients; add pasta and toss until evenly coated. Refrigerate until ready to serve.

Test Kitchen Tip: The nice thing about this salad is that you can make it in advance and have it ready and waiting whenever you want it. If the pasta absorbs some of the dressing while it sits, no worries, simply add a bit more and you're good to go!

Serving Suggestion:

If you're serving this for dinner, why not go all out and team it up with our Italian Three-Bean Soup on page 53 and the contest-winning recipe for Fabulous Ranch Cheese Bread on page 173? Now that's Italian!

RANCHER'S BBQ CHICKEN SALAD®

Serves 6

2 cups diced cooked chicken

¼ cup barbecue sauce

1 head romaine lettuce, chopped

2 tomatoes, diced

1 cup frozen corn, thawed

1 cup canned black beans, drained and rinsed

¼ cup diced red onion

½ cup shredded Monterey Jack cheese

1 cup tortilla chips, coarsely crushed

½ cup ranch dressing

1 In a medium bowl, combine chicken and barbecue sauce; toss until evenly coated.

2 Place lettuce on a large platter; top with chicken, tomato, corn, beans, onion, cheese, and tortilla chips. Pour Ranch dressing over salad and serve.

Fun Fact:

During Pat & Vanna's tour of the great city of Denver, they took a few minutes to enjoy the breathtaking views from one of the many ranches in the area. You can bet with the two of them, there was lots of horsin' around!

CROWD PLEASIN' COBB SALAD®

Serves 6

1 head iceberg lettuce, chopped

8 slices cooked bacon, crumbled

3 hard-boiled eggs, cut into wedges

1 avocado, peeled, pitted, and diced

2 tomatoes, diced

1 (2.25-ounce) can sliced black olives, drained

¼ pound blue cheese, crumbled

2 (¼-inch-thick) slices deli turkey, diced (about ½ lb)

2 (¼-inch-thick) slices deli ham, diced (about ½ lb)

1 cup Thousand Island dressing

1 Place the lettuce in a large bowl or on a platter. Arrange each topping in a section over lettuce. (See photo.)

2 Pour dressing over salad and serve.

Test Kitchen Tip: To make your own **Thousand Island Dressing**, simply mix together 2 cups mayo, ¼ cup ketchup, and ½ cup pickle relish that you drained really well. Then serve immediately or store in the fridge until ready to use.

Serving Suggestion:

What an easy weeknight dinner! It's packed with all sorts of goodness, and as always, feel free to mix and match the toppings to your family's personal tastes. And if you're feeling wheely creative, arrange the toppings like wedges on the Wheel. Talk about the ultimate Wheel watchers' salad. This is one recipe you won't stick your tongue out at, like Pat & Vanna did while goofing around on the set one day!

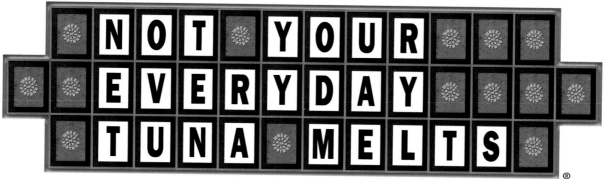

NOT YOUR EVERYDAY TUNA MELTS®

Serves 4

- 1 (12-ounce) can tuna, drained and flaked
- ½ cup mayonnaise
- 1 celery stalk, sliced
- 2 tablespoons finely chopped red onion
- ¼ teaspoon black pepper
- 8 slices tomato
- 4 slices rye bread
- 4 slices Havarti cheese
- ½ cup coarsely crushed potato chips

1 Preheat oven to 375 degrees F. Coat a baking sheet with cooking spray.

2 In a medium bowl, combine tuna, mayonnaise, celery, onion, and pepper; mix well.

3 Place 2 tomato slices on each slice of bread. Spread equal amounts of tuna mixture on tomatoes, and top with a slice of cheese. Sprinkle with potato chips. (Yes, on top of the cheese and yes, this is served open-faced.) Place on baking sheet.

4 Bake 10 minutes or until cheese is melted and the chips get extra crispy. Serve immediately.

Fun Fact:
Whether dinner is soup and a sandwich or a big feast, isn't it nice to know 5 nights a week you can always count on sitting down to dinner with Pat and Vanna? It's like having dinner with old friends. After all, they've been a dynamic duo since 1982.

WHARFSIDE SOURDOUGH PANINI ®

Serves 2

- 2 tablespoons honey mustard
- 4 slices sourdough bread
- ½ Granny Smith apple, thinly sliced
- ½ pound thinly sliced deli turkey breast
- 4 slices Swiss cheese
- 2 tablespoons butter, softened

1 Spread honey mustard evenly over one side of each slice of bread. Layer the sliced apple, turkey, and Swiss cheese on two slices of the bread. Top with remaining bread slices. Spread butter on both sides of each sandwich.

2 In a skillet or grill pan over medium heat, cook the sandwiches, pressing down on them with a spatula. Cook until golden and cheese is melted. Serve immediately.

Mix 'n' Match: Don't have Swiss? No problem! Maybe use creamy Havarti one time and pepper jack another to give it a kick.

On Location:

When the Wheel of Fortune or the Wheelmobile staff and crew go on the road, they love trying out the local fare. And while taping in San Francisco, you can bet they had their fair share of sourdough bread every which way ... from bread bowls brimming with clam chowder to grilled panini, just like this.

KIMBER'S DAD'S FAVORITE SANDWICH

Makes 1 sandwich

1 tablespoon butter

⅓ cup chopped green bell pepper

3 eggs

¼ teaspoon salt

⅛ teaspoon black pepper

2 tablespoons mayonnaise

2 slices whole wheat bread

1 In a small skillet over medium heat, melt butter. Add bell pepper and sauté 5 minutes, or until tender, stirring occasionally.

2 In a small bowl, whisk eggs, salt, and pepper and pour over bell pepper in skillet. Cook until eggs begin to set up, then lightly scramble and cook until eggs are firm.

3 Evenly spread mayonnaise on each slice of bread. Place eggs on one slice and top with second slice. Serve immediately.

Fun Fact:

"Have you ever noticed how good everyone on Wheel of Fortune looks? That's due to the very talented makeup crew. When I went on the show the first time, I had my makeup done by Kimber Eastwood. She was

the best—making me look great is no easy task. Later that afternoon, I found out that her dad is Clint Eastwood, as in "Make my day." We chatted about food and she shared with me what makes her dad's day when he comes over for a bite. It's her simple, but very tasty, fried pepper and egg sandwich that she says is his favorite."

*Howard Rosenthal,
On-Air Personality/Chief Food Officer
21 years at the Mr. Food Test Kitchen*

CLASSIC PHILLY CHEESESTEAKS®

Serves 4

3 tablespoons vegetable oil

2 large onions, thinly sliced

1-¼ pounds beef top round, thinly sliced

½ teaspoon black pepper

4 hoagie rolls, split

1 cup jarred cheese sauce, melted (Tested with Cheez Whiz)

1 In a large skillet over medium-high heat, heat oil. Add onions and sauté 5 to 7 minutes, or until tender; remove to a bowl and set aside.

2 Add beef to skillet and sprinkle with pepper; sauté 3 to 5 minutes, or until no pink remains. Remove beef to a cutting board, cut into very thin strips, then return to skillet. Add onions and cook 2 to 3 minutes, or until heated through.

3 Evenly divide the meat and onions onto each hoagie roll, drizzle with cheese, and serve immediately.

On Location:
If you're ever in Philly, you have to make sure you try at least one cheesesteak. They start off by slicing prime rib ultra thin and cooking it on the griddle. Then, they sorta chop it with their spatula until it looks almost shaved. This at-home way of doing it may not be traditional, but it gets the job done without ruining your skillet.

Game-Changing Poultry

SOUTHERN CRISPY FRIED CHICKEN ®

Serves 4

- 1 (3-½- to 4-pound) chicken, cut into 8 pieces
- 2 cups self-rising flour
- 2 teaspoons garlic powder
- 1 teaspoon paprika
- 2 teaspoons salt
- 1 teaspoon black pepper
- 3 eggs
- 1 tablespoon hot sauce
- 2 tablespoons water
- 2 cups vegetable oil

1 Place chicken in a large bowl of ice water; let sit 30 minutes.

2 In another large bowl, combine flour, garlic powder, paprika, salt, and pepper; mix well. In a third large bowl, mix eggs, hot sauce, and water. Remove chicken from ice water, shaking off excess. Dip in flour mixture, then in egg mixture, then back in flour mixture, coating completely each time.

3 In a large deep skillet over medium-low heat, heat oil until hot, but not smoking. Fry chicken in batches, 10 to 12 minutes per side, or until golden and no pink remains. Drain on a paper towel-lined platter. Serve immediately.

Test Kitchen Tip: If you have a thermometer, or an electric deep fryer or skillet, the ideal temperature to fry this is 350 degrees. The trick here is to make sure the chicken cooks through before the coating gets too dark.

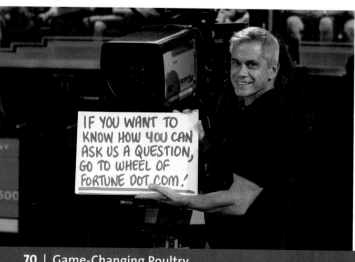

Behind the Scenes:

If you have questions on how to fry chicken or just want to chit-chat about food, go to www.MrFood.com. On the other hand, if you have a question about when Wheel of Fortune airs in your area, or how to audition to be a contestant, all you have to do is go to www.wheeloffortune.com.

Here, Bob Guzzi, the Cue Card Master for Wheel of Fortune for 13 years, holds up cue cards, which remind Pat and Vanna to mention all sorts of things during the show.

SUNDAY ROASTED CHICKEN

Serves 4

- 2 teaspoons salt
- 1 teaspoon paprika
- 1 teaspoon garlic powder
- ½ teaspoon onion powder
- ½ teaspoon dried ground thyme
- ¼ teaspoon black pepper
- ⅛ teaspoon cayenne pepper
- 1 (3-½- to 4-pound) chicken
- 1 onion, quartered

1 In a bowl, mix together salt, paprika, garlic powder, onion powder, thyme, black pepper, and cayenne pepper. Rub chicken inside and out with mixture. Place onion in cavity of chicken. Wrap chicken with plastic wrap and refrigerate at least 4 hours or overnight.

2 Preheat oven to 350 degrees F. Place chicken in a roasting pan. Bake uncovered 1-¼ hours, or until no longer pink in center. Let stand 5 minutes before carving.

Refrigerating this overnight with all the seasonings ensures that every bite is packed with flavor. And if you're wondering why we call this Sunday Roasted Chicken, it's because this is the perfect dish to roast on Sunday since it cooks nice and slow. And if by chance there are any leftovers, simply reheat them for dinner the next night, before flipping on Wheel of Fortune.

ALL-AMERICAN BARBECUE CHICKEN

Serves 4

1 (3-½- to 4-pound) chicken, cut into 8 pieces

½ teaspoon salt

½ teaspoon black pepper

1 cup ketchup

1 cup cola

¼ cup packed brown sugar

2 tablespoons Worchestershire sauce

1 tablespoon white vinegar

1 tablespoon butter

½ teaspoon garlic powder

¼ teaspoon cayenne pepper

1 Preheat oven to 375 degrees F. Coat a rimmed baking sheet with cooking spray. Place chicken on baking sheet and sprinkle evenly with salt and black pepper on both sides.

2 Roast chicken 30 minutes.

3 Meanwhile, in a saucepan over medium heat, combine remaining ingredients. Bring to a boil, then reduce heat and simmer 10 minutes, or until thickened. Reserve ½ cup barbecue sauce to serve with chicken.

4 Remove chicken from oven and brush with sauce. Return to oven and roast for an additional 30 minutes, or until no pink remains in chicken, basting occasionally. Serve with remaining barbecue sauce.

Did You Know?

This recipe is so good it's bound to become a coast-to-coast favorite, just like the show. Since 1988, Wheel of Fortune has taped shows on location more than 60 times and in more than 25 cities. Now that's All-American!

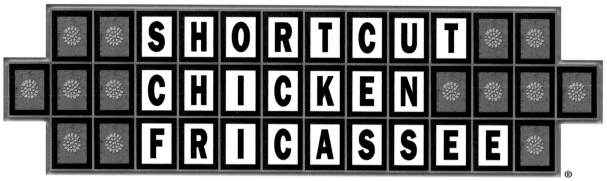

SHORTCUT CHICKEN FRICASSEE ®

Serves 4

2 tablespoons vegetable oil

1 (3-½- to 4-pound) chicken, cut into 8 pieces

1 onion, chopped

2 carrots, coarsely chopped

1 (10-¾-ounce) can cream of mushroom soup

½ cup milk

1 tablespoon lemon juice

¼ teaspoon ground thyme

½ teaspoon salt

¼ teaspoon black pepper

1 In a large skillet over medium-high heat, heat oil; cook chicken 10 to 12 minutes, or until browned. Remove to a platter.

2 Add onion and carrots to skillet; sauté 3 to 4 minutes, or until onion is soft.

3 Meanwhile, in a medium bowl, whisk together soup, milk, lemon juice, thyme, salt, and pepper.

4 Return chicken to skillet, pour soup mixture over chicken, and cover. Reduce heat to low and simmer about 30 minutes, or until chicken is no longer pink and juices run clear.

Serving Suggestion:
To make this a complete fill-ya-up meal, why not serve it over some quick-cooking rice or curly noodles? That way you won't miss a bit of the flavor-packed sauce.

MICHELLE'S MEMORY-MAKING CHICKEN

Serves 4

1 (3-½- to 4-pound) chicken

Salt & pepper for sprinkling

1 whole head garlic, cut in half

1 lemon, cut in half

1 loaf Brioche bread (or egg bread), torn into 1-inch pieces (about 4 cups)

1 Preheat oven to 425 degrees F. Rinse chicken inside and out with cold water and pat dry. Carefully slide fingers between the skin and the breast, separating it, and being careful not to tear skin.

2 Season inside of chicken with salt and pepper, and place garlic and lemon in the cavity. Stuff bread under skin, covering breast meat and being careful not to tear skin. Secure skin with a toothpick. Tuck legs underneath each other to secure, or tie with string. Place in roasting pan. Generously season outside of chicken with salt and pepper.

3 Roast, uncovered, 45 minutes. Remove from the oven, cover loosely with foil, and roast 25 to 30 more minutes, or until internal temperature reaches 165 degrees and no pink remains.

Behind the Recipe:

Michelle Loewenstein, the first Wheel of Fortune million dollar winner, says the one dish her family likes the most is her roasted chicken. After the Test Kitchen made it, there was no question why they love it so much.

It's super moist, and as the bread roasts with the chicken, it becomes super tasty. And if you're wondering what she felt like being a million dollar winner..."I felt like a million bucks!! Haha! It was a life-changing moment and a memory that I will never forget. It's still surreal all these years later. Now, my 4-year-old recognizes the show and will tell me that's the game show I was on. It's still my favorite. Thank you for such an amazing memory!"

Michelle Loewenstein
Los Angeles, CA

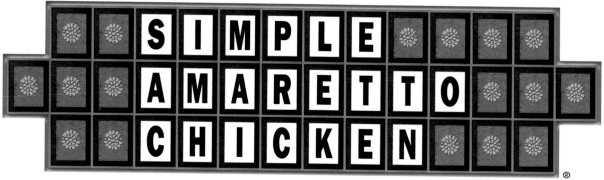

SIMPLE AMARETTO CHICKEN

Serves 4

1 cup panko bread crumbs

½ cup finely chopped almonds

2 tablespoons sugar

1 teaspoon cinnamon

1-½ teaspoons salt

1 egg

4 boneless, skinless chicken breasts

2 tablespoons butter

2 tablespoons vegetable oil

1 cup orange marmalade

2 tablespoons amaretto (almond) liqueur

Sliced almonds for garnish (optional)

1 In a shallow dish, combine bread crumbs, chopped almonds, sugar, cinnamon, and salt; mix well. In another shallow dish, beat egg.

2 In a large skillet over medium-low heat, place butter and oil. Dip chicken in egg, then in bread crumb mixture, coating both sides completely. Sauté 6 to 8 minutes per side, or until golden brown and the inside is no longer pink.

3 Meanwhile, in a small saucepan over low heat, combine marmalade and liqueur; heat until warm. Serve over chicken and sprinkle with sliced almonds, if desired.

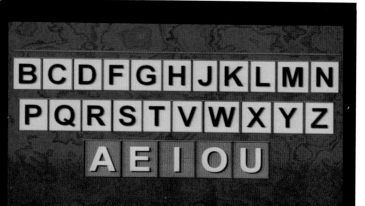

Behind the Scenes:

If you've ever wondered how the contestants know which letters have been called out in a round, let us fill you in. There's a board that faces the players (no, you won't see this on TV at home) and displays all the letters that haven't been called yet. This is a huge help—especially when contestants are trying to solve the puzzle, look relaxed on national TV, and are standing just feet away from Pat and Vanna. Can you imagine?

SKILLET PEPPERONI CHICKEN

Serves 4

4 boneless, skinless chicken breasts

Salt and pepper for sprinkling

1 tablespoon olive oil

1 (10.5-ounce) can condensed cream of chicken soup

¾ cup half-and-half

2 tomatoes, chopped

¼ cup sliced pepperoni, cut in quarters

1 teaspoon garlic powder

½ teaspoon Italian seasoning

½ teaspoon onion powder

1 Lightly sprinkle chicken with salt and pepper.

2 In a large skillet over medium-high heat, heat oil until hot. Sauté chicken 6 to 8 minutes per side, or until browned on both sides and no pink remains in center. Remove chicken to a plate, cover, and set aside.

3 In the same skillet over medium heat, combine remaining ingredients and cook 5 minutes, or until hot. Add chicken back into pan and cook 3 to 5 minutes, or until heated through. Serve immediately.

If you thought pepperoni only goes on top of pizza, think again. You see, pepperoni is packed with so much flavor that when it's simmered in a sauce like this, all that goodness blends into the sauce and adds a whole new dimension to this easy weeknight favorite.

CHINATOWN SWEET & SOUR CHICKEN

Serves 4

1 cup apple cider vinegar

½ cup ketchup

2 tablespoons soy sauce

1-½ cups sugar

1 teaspoon garlic powder

1 green bell pepper, cut into 1-inch chunks

1 (20-ounce) can pineapple chunks, drained

6 maraschino cherries, halved

3 eggs

1-½ pounds boneless, skinless chicken breasts, cut into 1-inch chunks

½ teaspoon salt

¼ teaspoon black pepper

⅓ cup cornstarch

1-½ cups vegetable oil

1 tablespoon sesame seeds

1 In a large saucepan over medium heat, combine vinegar, ketchup, soy sauce, sugar, and garlic powder; cook 10 to 12 minutes, or until mixture is thickened. Stir in green pepper, pineapple, and cherries, reduce heat, and simmer 10 minutes.

2 In a bowl, whisk eggs. In a large bowl, combine chicken, salt, and pepper. Add cornstarch and toss until evenly coated. Dip chicken, a few pieces at a time, into the egg, coating evenly.

3 Meanwhile, in a large skillet over medium heat, heat oil until hot, but not smoking. Place chicken in the skillet and cook 2 to 3 minutes, or until golden on all sides and no pink remains in the center. Remove to a paper towel-lined plate. Repeat with remaining chicken. Toss chicken with sauce, sprinkle with sesame seeds, and serve.

Behind the Recipe:

Over the years, as the show and the Wheelmobile have traveled the country, you can bet the staff and crew have had lots of Chinese takeout. You can recreate takeout fun at home with this "takeout fake-out" dish that is Chinatown-worthy.

STUFFED CHICKEN CAPRESE

Serves 4

4 boneless skinless chicken breasts

1 tablespoon Italian seasoning, divided

Salt and pepper for sprinkling

1 (12-ounce) jar roasted red peppers, drained and sliced

4 large basil leaves plus extra sliced for garnish

1 (8-ounce) piece fresh mozzarella cheese, cut into 8 slices, divided

1 tablespoon grated Parmesan cheese

Olive oil for drizzling

1 Preheat oven to 350 degrees F. Coat a baking sheet with cooking spray.

2 Place chicken on a cutting board and butterfly by slicing into the long edge of the breasts horizontally, stopping just about ¼-inch from the opposite side. On the baking sheet, open each chicken breast like a book. Sprinkle with ½ the Italian seasoning, the salt, and pepper.

3 Layer roasted red pepper, a basil leaf, and 1 slice of cheese on one side of the chicken. Fold the other flap of the chicken over, tucking in the filling as necessary. Sprinkle with remaining Italian seasoning.

4 Bake chicken 25 to 30 minutes, or until no longer pink. Top with remaining mozzarella and sprinkle with Parmesan cheese. Bake 5 additional minutes, or until cheese begins to melt. Sprinkle with sliced basil and drizzle evenly with olive oil. Serve immediately.

Test Kitchen. Mr. Food Hints & Tips

If you've never butterflied a chicken breast before and would like to watch a step-by-step video, simply go to MrFood.com and click on the "How-To Videos" tab. There you'll be able to learn all sorts of tips and tricks that will make you a kitchen hero in no time.

SUPER-FAST CHICKEN®

Serves 4

2 cups crispy rice cereal

1 teaspoon paprika

1 teaspoon salt

½ teaspoon black pepper

¼ cup mayonnaise

4 boneless, skinless chicken breasts

1 Preheat oven to 350 degrees F. Coat a baking sheet with cooking spray.

2 In a resealable plastic bag, combine cereal, paprika, salt, and pepper; mix well. Place mayonnaise in a shallow dish. Add 1 chicken breast and turn to coat evenly with mayonnaise, then place in bag with cereal mixture and shake until evenly coated on all sides. Place on baking sheet. Repeat with remaining chicken. Bake 25 minutes, or until crispy and no pink remains in center.

Serving Suggestion: The kids will love the simplicity of this, but to give it a grownup blast of flavor, try serving it with a **Chipotle Mayo Dipping Sauce**. Just mix ½ cup mayonnaise, ½ cup sour cream, 1 finely chopped canned chipotle pepper, ¼ teaspoon garlic powder, and ¼ teaspoon salt.

Behind the Recipe:

This recipe was inspired by Debbie Williams, Assistant to the Line Producer, Randy Berke, who says this is one of her family's favorites. Being an active mom and working at the show for more than 14 years, Debbie learned that she needs dinners that are super fast, hence the name. Not only does her family love it, so does Randy when she brings in leftovers for lunch and shares them with him. Thank you, Debbie, for sharing this with us!

GARLICKY CHICKEN PARMESAN

Serves 4

1 (26-ounce) jar spaghetti sauce

2 cloves garlic, minced

1 cup Italian bread crumbs

1-½ teaspoons garlic powder

2 eggs

1 tablespoon water

4 boneless, skinless chicken breasts, flattened to a ¼-inch

Salt & pepper for sprinkling

¼ cup vegetable oil

1 cup shredded mozzarella cheese

Parmesan cheese for sprinkling

1 Preheat oven to 350 degrees F. Coat a baking sheet with cooking spray. In a medium saucepan over low heat, combine spaghetti sauce and minced garlic, and simmer until ready to use.

2 In a shallow dish, combine bread crumbs and garlic powder. In another shallow dish, whisk eggs and water. Evenly sprinkle both sides of chicken with salt and pepper.

3 In a large skillet over medium-high heat, heat oil until hot, but not smoking. Dip chicken in egg mixture, then in bread crumbs, until evenly coated. Sauté chicken 5 to 6 minutes, or until no pink remains and chicken is golden brown, turning halfway through. Remove to the baking sheet; repeat with remaining chicken.

4 Evenly spoon sauce over chicken, then sprinkle with mozzarella and Parmesan cheeses. Bake 8 to 10 minutes, or until cheese is melted.

Behind the Recipe:

If you love chicken Parmesan, then you'll go bonkers over this oven-baked version of the Italian classic. The coating is super-crispy and the chicken is juicy—bite after bite. And if that's not enough, the fact that it's smothered in a rich garlicky tomato sauce and then finished with not one, but two Italian cheeses will make you put this at the top of your "what-to-make-for-dinner" list.

EASY PEASY ARTICHOKE CHICKEN

Serves 4

1 (14-ounce) can artichoke hearts in water, drained and chopped

½ cup grated Parmesan cheese

¾ cup mayonnaise

1 teaspoon garlic powder

4 boneless, skinless chicken breasts

1 Preheat oven to 375 degrees F. Coat a 9- x 13-inch baking dish with cooking spray.

2 In a medium bowl, combine artichokes, Parmesan cheese, mayonnaise, and garlic powder. Place chicken in baking dish and spread artichoke mixture over top.

3 Bake 30 to 35 minutes, or until no pink remains in chicken and juices run clear.

RECIPE CONTEST WINNER

"I was looking for something quick, easy, yet still delicious, so we would not miss any of Wheel, which is a daily ritual in our house. Since we love artichokes and cheese, this blend of flavors is a real hit at our house. I've shared this with many people and they all love it."

Lilly Dalsin
Springfield, IL

INDIAN CURRY IN A HURRY

Serves 4

3 tablespoons vegetable oil

1 onion, coarsely chopped

3 cloves garlic, chopped

3 tablespoons curry powder

1 teaspoon cinnamon

1 teaspoon paprika

1 teaspoon salt

1 teaspoon sugar

½ teaspoon grated fresh ginger

1 cup plain yogurt

¾ cup coconut milk

1 tablespoon tomato paste

2 pounds boneless, skinless chicken breasts, cut into 1-inch chunks

2 tablespoons lemon juice

⅛ teaspoon cayenne pepper

½ cup frozen peas, thawed

1 In a large skillet over medium heat, heat oil. Add onion and sauté until golden. Stir in garlic, curry powder, cinnamon, paprika, salt, sugar, and ginger; continue stirring one minute. Add yogurt, coconut milk, and tomato paste, stirring until well combined.

2 Add the chicken, stir, and bring to a boil, then reduce heat to low and simmer 15 to 20 minutes, or until chicken is cooked through and no pink remains.

3 Stir in lemon juice, cayenne pepper, and peas; simmer 5 minutes, or until mixture is heated through.

Serving Suggestion:
This is best served over basmati rice or naan (Indian flatbread) so you don't miss any of the flavor-packed sauce! If you don't have fresh ginger, you can substitute ¼ teaspoon ground ginger. And if this recipe looks familiar, it's because Howard, from the Mr. Food Test Kitchen, made it for Pat and Vanna during a recent Fabulous Food week. Rumor has it that Pat went back for seconds, so you know it's gotta be good!

CHEESE AND CRACKERS CHICKEN

Serves 4

- 1 cup finely crushed butter crackers
- ½ teaspoon paprika
- 4 boneless, skinless chicken breasts
- ⅛ teaspoon salt plus extra for sprinkling
- ⅛ teaspoon black pepper plus extra for sprinkling
- 4 slices Swiss cheese
- ½ stick butter
- ¾ cup dry white wine

1 Preheat oven to 375 degrees F. Coat a 9- x 13-inch baking dish with cooking spray.

2 Combine crushed crackers and paprika in a shallow dish. Evenly sprinkle chicken with salt and pepper, then place in crumb mixture, coating evenly on both sides. Place chicken in baking dish.

3 Bake 20 minutes, remove from oven, and place slice of cheese on each breast. Return to oven and cook 5 to 10 more minutes, or until no pink remains in chicken.

4 Meanwhile, in a small skillet over medium-high heat, melt butter; add wine, the ⅛ teaspoon salt, and the ⅛ teaspoon pepper, and simmer until reduced slightly. Pour over chicken and serve.

The Test Kitchen loves to combine the flavors and textures of everyday ingredients to make something new and unexpected. Here they team everyone's favorite, cheese and crackers, with chicken to make them very fancy-schmancy. All you need is a glass of wine and you're good to go.

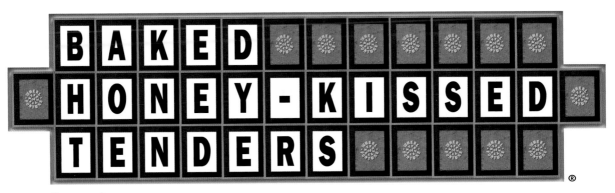

BAKED HONEY-KISSED TENDERS

Serves 4

3 cups cornflakes, finely crushed

2 tablespoons sugar

½ teaspoon cinnamon

1 teaspoon salt

½ cup milk

1 egg

1 teaspoon hot sauce

1-½ pounds chicken tenders

Cooking spray

½ cup honey

1 tablespoon butter

1 Preheat oven to 375 degrees F. Coat a baking sheet with cooking spray.

2 In a shallow dish, combine cornflakes, sugar, cinnamon, and salt; mix well. In another shallow dish, combine milk, egg, and hot sauce; mix well.

3 Dip chicken tenders into milk mixture, then roll in cereal mixture, coating completely. Place on baking sheet, repeating until all tenders are coated. Evenly spray with cooking spray. Bake 18 to 20 minutes, or until chicken is no longer pink in center.

4 Meanwhile, in a small microwaveable bowl, combine honey and butter; heat 1 minute, or until butter is melted and honey is warm. Serve as a dipping sauce or drizzle over chicken.

Did You Know?

These crispy crunchy tenders are perfect to nibble on while watching Wheel, 'cause you can pick them up with your hands. The combo of the honey dipping sauce with the slightly honey-kissed coating makes these so good you'll definitely want to add these to your weeknight dinner routine.

LITTLE ITALY CHICKEN CACCIATORE®

Serves 4

8 chicken thighs

½ teaspoon salt

½ teaspoon black pepper

2 teaspoons olive oil

1 onion, cut into chunks

1 green bell pepper, cut into chunks

2 cloves garlic, minced

½ cup beef broth

1 (14-½-ounce) can Italian-style diced tomatoes, undrained

1 Season chicken evenly with salt and pepper. In a large deep skillet over medium-high heat, heat oil; add chicken and cook 5 minutes per side, or until lightly browned. Remove from skillet and set aside.

2 Add onion and green pepper to skillet and sauté 5 minutes. Return chicken to skillet; add garlic, broth, and tomatoes, and bring to a boil. Cover, reduce heat to low, and simmer 10 minutes. Uncover and simmer an additional 10 minutes, or until chicken is cooked through. Serve topped with sauce.

Test Kitchen Tip: If you prefer white meat rather than dark, feel free to use boneless chicken breasts instead. If you do, just keep in mind that you may need to simmer it a couple of extra minutes based on how large they are.

Serving Suggestion:
With a sauce this good, you'll want to serve this over some fluffy cooked rice or with some crusty bread, so you don't leave behind a bit of this flavor-packed sauce. If you do a good enough job, you can almost skip washing the dishes!

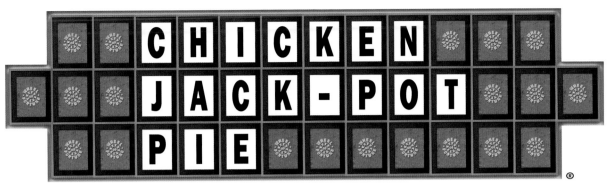

CHICKEN JACK-POT PIE

Serves 6

2 (10.75-ounce) cans cream of chicken soup, undiluted

1 cup half-and-half

¼ teaspoon poultry seasoning

½ teaspoon salt

¼ teaspoon black pepper

2 cups frozen mixed vegetables

3 cups pulled cooked rotisserie chicken

1 sheet frozen puff pastry, thawed, and refrigerated until ready to use

1 Preheat oven to 400 degrees F.

2 In a large skillet over medium heat, combine soup, half-and-half, poultry seasoning, salt, and pepper; mix well. Stir in vegetables and chicken and cook 5 minutes, just until hot.

3 Pour into a 9-inch deep dish pie plate. Place puff pastry over top, trimming to fit, and press the edges to seal. Bake on a baking sheet, 20 to 25 minutes, or until puff pastry is golden. (This way if it bubbles over, it won't make a mess.)

If you want to cut the puff pastry before filling the pie plate, put the pastry on a cutting board, turn the empty pie plate upside-down over it, then run a knife around the edge. Voila, the perfect size! Now that's what we call super easy.

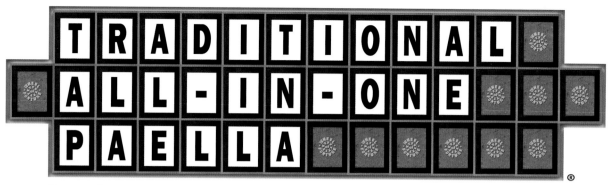

TRADITIONAL ALL-IN-ONE PAELLA®

Serves 6

- 1 (10-ounce) package yellow rice
- 1 tablespoon olive oil
- 1 pound boneless, skinless chicken thighs, cut into 1-inch chunks
- ½ pound chorizo sausage, cut into ¼-inch slices
- 1 cup chicken broth
- 1 red and 1 green bell pepper, cut into ½-inch chunks
- ½ cup chopped onion
- 2 cups frozen peas
- 1 pound frozen shrimp, peeled and deveined, thawed
- 1 teaspoon paprika
- 1 teaspoon kosher salt

1 Cook the rice according to package directions; set aside.

2 In a large skillet over medium-high heat, heat oil. Add chicken and sausage; cook 5 to 7 minutes, or until browned. Transfer to a plate.

3 In the same skillet, add broth; bring to a simmer. Add bell peppers, onion, and peas. Cook 4 to 6 minutes, or until heated through, stirring occasionally. Add shrimp; cook 2 to 4 minutes, or until pink. Stir in paprika, salt, and cooked rice. Return chicken and sausage to the skillet; reduce heat to medium and cook until heated through. Serve immediately.

Behind the Scenes:

One of the secrets to keeping the show fresh is a constantly changing theme. Every week there's a new one. And one of the favorites is Fabulous Food week. After all, who doesn't love food? You can bet Pat and Vanna love it when Howard, from the Mr. Food Test Kitchen, comes on the show and shares a dish with them. Here, Pat and Vanna are about to dig into some paella to salute the fabulous food of Spain. There were probably lots of viewers that night wishing they could reach right into their TV to sneak a forkful!

AMISH-STYLE CHICKEN CASSEROLE

Serves 10

1 pound medium egg noodles

2 (10-½-ounce) cans cream of mushroom soup

2 cups milk

1 stick butter, melted

1 (2-ounce) box onion soup mix (use 2 envelopes)

2 (10-ounce) packages frozen chopped spinach, thawed and well-drained

8 ounces mushrooms, sliced

3 cups shredded rotisserie chicken

2 cups shredded Swiss cheese, divided

1 Preheat oven to 350 degrees F. Coat a 9- x 13-inch baking dish with cooking spray.

2 In a large pot of boiling water, cook noodles according to package directions; drain.

3 In a large bowl, combine all ingredients except ½ cup Swiss cheese. Place mixture in baking dish and cover with aluminum foil. Bake 35 to 40 minutes, or until hot in center. Sprinkle with remaining cheese and cook 5 additional minutes, or until cheese is melted.

Fun Fact:

If you're thinking, "What makes this Amish-Style?" it's the fact that this dish is inspired by the all-in-one type of simplistic cooking that the Amish are known for. The big difference is that here, the recipe uses a bunch of shortcut ingredients to get a hot meal on the table in no time, rather than starting everything from scratch.

MEXI-CHICKEN STUFFED SHELLS

Serves 6

1 (12-ounce) package jumbo pasta shells

1 (8-ounce) package cream cheese, softened

3 cloves garlic, minced

1 teaspoon ground cumin

1 tablespoon chopped fresh cilantro

½ teaspoon salt

¼ teaspoon black pepper

2 cups shredded mozzarella cheese, divided

1 (15-ounce) can black beans, drained and rinsed

2 cups frozen corn, thawed

2 cups chopped cooked chicken

1 (24-ounce) jar salsa, divided

1 Preheat oven to 375 degrees F. Coat a 9- x 13-inch baking dish with cooking spray. Cook pasta shells according to package directions; drain and set aside to cool.

2 In a large bowl, combine cream cheese, garlic, cumin, cilantro, salt, pepper, and 1 cup mozzarella cheese. Stir in black beans, corn, and chicken; mix well.

3 Pour 1 cup salsa in bottom of baking dish. Evenly fill shells with chicken mixture and place in baking dish. Pour remaining salsa over shells and cover with aluminum foil.

4 Bake 35 to 40 minutes, or until hot in center. Remove foil, top with remaining mozzarella cheese, and bake 5 to 10 additional minutes, or until cheese is melted.

Did You Know?

Merv Griffin, the creator of Wheel of Fortune, hired Vanna based on the chemistry she had with host Pat Sajak during her audition. They blend so well, just like the flavors do in this unexpectedly delicious twist on stuffed shells. Kudos to Patty in the Mr. Food Test Kitchen for putting this combo together. And thank you, Merv, for one of America's favorite duos!

STACKED ENCHILADA CASSEROLE®

Serves 6

Ingredients:

- 2 (15-ounce) cans black beans, rinsed and drained
- 1 (16-ounce) package frozen corn, thawed
- 4 cups shredded cooked chicken
- 6 scallions, thinly sliced, divided
- 2 (10-ounce) cans red enchilada sauce
- 16 corn tortillas, cut into strips
- 3 cups shredded Mexican blend cheese
- 1 avocado, diced
- 2 tablespoons chopped fresh cilantro

1 Preheat oven to 375 degrees F. Coat a 9- x 13-inch baking dish with cooking spray.

2 In a large bowl, combine black beans, corn, chicken, and 4 scallions. Mix until well combined. Pour about ¼ of the enchilada sauce evenly in bottom of baking dish. Layer ¼ of the tortilla strips over sauce. Layer with ⅓ of the chicken mixture, then ¼ of the cheese. Repeat with another ¼ of the enchilada sauce, ¼ of tortilla strips and ⅓ of chicken mixture. Repeat with another layer of each. Finally, layer with the remaining tortilla strips and spoon sauce over the top. Cover with foil and bake 20 minutes.

3 Remove pan from oven and remove foil. Sprinkle with remaining cheese and bake, uncovered, 10 more minutes, or until cheese is melted. Top with avocado, cilantro, and remaining scallions. Serve immediately.

Fun Fact:

Vanna holds the Guinness World Record for "Most Frequent Clapper." She puts her hands together for contestants more than 600 times each night—that's over 3.7 million claps during the last 32 seasons. For that record and so much more, Vanna deserves a big round of applause!

TURKEY MUFFIN TIN MEATLOAVES

Makes 12 mini-meatloaves

2 pounds ground turkey

½ cup chopped onion

1 cup crushed butter crackers

½ cup milk

1 egg

1 teaspoon garlic powder

1-½ teaspoons salt

½ teaspoon black pepper

½ cup ketchup

¼ cup brown sugar

1 Preheat oven to 350 degrees F. Coat a 12-cup muffin tin with cooking spray.

2 In a large bowl, combine all ingredients except ketchup and brown sugar; mix well. Evenly divide the turkey mixture into each muffin cup. In a small bowl, mix ketchup and brown sugar. Place a spoonful of ketchup mixture over each mini meatloaf.

3 Bake 30 to 35 minutes, or until the center is no longer pink. Let sit 5 minutes before removing from the pan and serving.

Test Kitchen Mr. Food Hints & Tips

If you're trying to get dinner on the table quickly, then these muffin-sized meatloaves are perfect. You see, since they are so much smaller than a traditional meatloaf, they cook up in about half the time. And the best part is that everyone gets their very own.

TURKEY 'N' TRIMMINGS ROLL-UPS®

Serves 5

- 2 (12-ounce) jars turkey gravy
- 1 (8-ounce) package herb stuffing
- ½ cup dried cranberries
- 1-¾ cups chicken broth
- 10 (1/8-inch-thick) slices deli turkey breast

1 Preheat oven to 350 degrees F. Coat a 9- x 13-inch baking dish with cooking spray.

2 Pour half the jar of gravy in baking dish; set aside.

3 In a large bowl, combine stuffing, cranberries, and broth; mix well. Place turkey slices on the counter and spoon stuffing mixture evenly in the center of each slice. Roll up crepe-style and place seam-side down in baking dish. Pour remaining gravy over roll-ups and cover with aluminum foil.

4 Bake 30 to 35 minutes, or until heated through. Serve each roll-up with gravy from the pan.

Test Kitchen. Mr. Food Hints & Tips

If you love turkey with all the fixin's, but hate waiting a whole year until Thanksgiving rolls around, then this is one recipe that you'll be thankful for. It has all the taste of a traditional turkey day feast— without all the work. That means in about 45 minutes you can be sitting down in front of the TV watching Wheel with a dinner that is so good, you'll gobble it up.

Bonus Round Beef & Pork

HARRY'S HOTLINE CHILI

Serves 8

2 pounds ground beef

1-½ cups chopped onion

3 cloves garlic, minced

1 (28-ounce) can crushed tomatoes

2 (16-ounce) cans red kidney beans, drained

⅓ cup chili powder

1 teaspoon ground cumin

1 teaspoon salt

1 teaspoon black pepper

1 In a large pot over medium-high heat, sauté beef, onion, and garlic 8 to 10 minutes, or until no pink remains in the beef; drain off excess liquid.

2 Add remaining ingredients; mix well. Cover, reduce heat to low, and simmer 45 minutes, stirring occasionally.

Test Kitchen Tip: If you like your chili spicier, feel free to add a few shakes of hot pepper sauce right at the end. Just don't overdo it or you'll be as red as the hotline phone.

Behind the Recipe:

Harry Friedman, Executive Producer of Wheel of Fortune, says one of his favorite kick-back-and-relax type of meals has to be a bowl of hearty chili. So, after he shared with the Test Kitchen what he likes in his chili, they created one based on his inspiration. And is it ever amazing!

If you ever get the chance to attend a live taping of the show, here's a hint on how to recognize Harry … he's the one sitting at the producer's table, just a few feet from the Wheel, with the big red telephone in front of him. That's the hotline to the control room.

GRANDMA ROSE'S STUFFED CABBAGE

Serves 6

1 large cabbage, cored

1 (28-ounce) can crushed tomatoes, undrained

½ cup light brown sugar

1 tablespoon Worcestershire sauce

2 tablespoons lemon juice

1 pound ground beef

1 cup cooked rice, cooled

1 small onion, chopped

1 egg

1 teaspoon celery salt

½ teaspoon salt

½ teaspoon black pepper

1 In a large saucepan over high heat, bring 1 inch of water to a boil. Place cabbage in water, core-side down; cover and reduce heat to low. Steam 20 minutes, or until cabbage leaves pull apart easily. Drain and set aside to cool slightly.

2 Preheat oven to 350 degrees F. Coat a 9- x 13-inch baking dish with cooking spray.

3 In a bowl, combine tomatoes, brown sugar, Worcestershire sauce, and lemon juice; mix well and set aside. In a large bowl, combine beef, rice, onion, egg, celery salt, salt, pepper, and 2 tablespoons tomato mixture; mix well. Place 1 cup tomato mixture in bottom of baking dish.

4 Carefully peel the cabbage leaves off head and remove thick stems. Place about ¼ cup of meat mixture in center of each leaf. Starting at the core end, loosely roll up each leaf, folding in the sides. Place seam side down in baking dish. Spoon remaining sauce over top of cabbage rolls and cover with aluminum foil.

5 Bake 1-¼ hours. Uncover and cook 10 to 15 additional minutes, or until the cabbage is tender and the beef is cooked through.

Behind the Recipe:

"I remember visiting my grandmother in the early 80's and watching what she called her 'new game show.' (It was the evening version of Wheel of Fortune, which launched in 1983.) She would make a pan of stuffed cabbage (my favorite), and we would eat while watching Wheel. Of course, we had to adjust the rabbit ears until we got a good picture. Those are some of my best memories. I can only hope that by sharing her recipe, you, too, will be able to create memories as special as these are to me."

Howard Rosenthal
On-Air Personality/Chief Food Officer
21 years at Mr. Food Test Kitchen

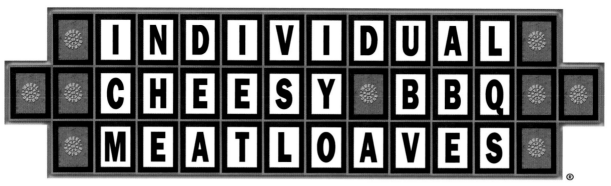

INDIVIDUAL CHEESY BBQ MEATLOAVES

Serves 6

1-¼ cups shredded sharp Cheddar cheese, divided

2 scallions, sliced

2 pounds lean ground beef

3 slices white bread, torn into small pieces

2 eggs

1-¼ cups barbecue sauce, divided

1 teaspoon salt

¼ teaspoon black pepper

1 Preheat oven to 350 degrees F. Coat a baking sheet with cooking spray.

2 In a small bowl, combine ¾ cup cheese and the scallions; mix well and set aside.

3 In a large bowl, combine ground beef, bread, eggs, ¾ cup barbecue sauce, salt, and pepper. With your hands, mix well. Divide into 6 equal portions and place each on a 10-inch long piece of wax paper and pat firmly into a 4- x 6-inch rectangle. Sprinkle 2 tablespoons cheese mixture evenly over ground beef. Roll up jelly roll-style starting from the short end, by lifting wax paper and removing the paper as you roll. Gently pinch the ends of the meat to seal. Place seam-side down on baking sheet. Repeat with remaining meat and cheese.

4 Spoon 1 tablespoon barbecue sauce over each and bake 25 minutes. Remove from oven, sprinkle with remaining cheese, and bake for 5 more minutes, or until no pink remains. Allow to stand 5 minutes before serving

Over the years, the Test Kitchen has created many varieties of meatloaf. Everything from all-American and ethnic ones, to one that was frosted with mashed potatoes and looked just like a cake! But never before has it churned out individual-sized ones that ooze with cheese and are finished with lip-smackin' BBQ sauce. Why oh why did they wait so long? Nevermind that—it was worth the wait. Now the question is...why should you wait any longer?

CHARLIE'S KICKIN' MEATLOAF

Serves 6

1-½ pounds lean ground beef

1 teaspoon salt

¼ teaspoon black pepper

1 (14.5-ounce) can diced tomatoes with green chilies

½ cup chopped onion

½ cup chopped green bell pepper

1 cup quick-cooking oats

1 egg

½ cup ketchup

2 tablespoons brown sugar

1 tablespoon mustard

1 Preheat oven to 350 degrees F. Coat a 9- x 13-inch baking dish with cooking spray.

2 In a bowl, combine ground beef, salt, black pepper, tomatoes, onion, bell pepper, oats, and egg. Shape into a loaf and place in baking dish.

3 In a small bowl, mix ketchup, brown sugar, and mustard; spread over loaf.

4 Bake 1 to 1-¼ hours, or until no pink remains.

RECIPE CONTEST WINNER

"For years, I tried making meatloaf for my husband and after many attempts, I finally came up with this winning recipe! My husband LOVES this meatloaf since it's so moist and has a slight kick from the green chilies. And before baking, I often top it with thinly sliced green pepper rings. Since my husband's name is Charlie, I couldn't think of a better name for this dish than 'Charlie's Kickin' Meatloaf.'"

Lisa Robinson
Broken Arrow, OK

CHAMPIONSHIP MATCH LOCO MOCO

Serves 2

- 2 hamburger patties
- 2 cups cooked rice, warmed
- 2 eggs
- ½ cup beef gravy

1 In a large skillet over medium heat, cook hamburger patties 8 to 10 minutes, or to desired doneness, turning once.

2 Evenly divide rice onto 2 plates, then top with hamburgers; cover to keep warm.

3 Wipe out skillet, then coat with cooking spray. Cook eggs sunny side up 2 to 3 minutes, or until whites are set.

4 Place eggs over hamburgers and top with gravy. Serve immediately.

Behind the Recipe:

If you're thinking, "What's Loco Moco?" this will help you out. Legend has it that this fill-ya-up dish has been around since the 1940's when a restaurant owner on the Big Island of Hawaii created a dish that was

inexpensive to feed the local kids. It was steamed rice topped with a hamburger and a fried egg, smothered in gravy. As she was about to put it on her menu board, she didn't know what to call it, so she asked her husband. He said, "Let's call it 'Loco Moco' since the kids are crazy." The name stuck, and today, Loco Moco is known as the ultimate Hawaiian comfort food.

"I had the fortune of solving the puzzle 'CHAMPIONSHIP MATCH' with a single 'T'. Following the broadcast, I received an enormous amount of congratulations from fans of the show and the subsequent viral video, which has been flattering and heart-warming. The funny thing is my name is now unofficially the puzzle that I solved. When I'm recognized by someone, greeted by a fan, or tell someone that I was on the show, the response is always "You're 'Championship Match'?"

"My nickname is even more amusing on days that I wear the unique Aloha attire from the show. I've had several fans say "It's him. It's 'The Shirt!'" The shirt has literally garnered its own fame.

"So, I - Rufus "Championship Match" "The Shirt" Cumberlander - would like to say mahalo to all the fans of the show for your kind words and support. I sincerely appreciate you all — no matter what you call me."

Rufus Cumberlander,
One Letter Puzzle-Solver
Ewa Beach, HI

(All Pat could say to Rufus after his amazing solve was: "Somebody ... put somethin' in the Loco Moco!")

Jim Thorton is the official Announcer of Wheel of Fortune. Although you don't see him often, you can recognize his upbeat voice. It's been said you can tell if someone is smiling when they talk, and with Jim, it's apparent he's always smiling.

JIM'S WEST VIRGINIA HOTDOG SAUCE

Makes 4 cups

- 1 pound ground beef
- 1 (15-ounce) can tomato sauce
- 2 tablespoons red wine vinegar
- ¾ cup water
- ½ cup finely chopped onion
- 1 tablespoon olive oil
- 1-½ teaspoons prepared mustard
- 1-½ teaspoons onion powder
- 1-½ teaspoons garlic powder
- ½ teaspoon Worcestershire sauce
- 1-¼ teaspoons chili powder
- ½ teaspoon paprika
- ¼ teaspoon cumin
- ¼ teaspoon hot sauce, or to taste
- ½ teaspoon salt
- ¼ teaspoon black pepper
- 1 (6-ounce) can tomato paste

1 In a large pot, combine all ingredients; mix well. (Do NOT brown the meat first; this keeps the texture of the finished product smooth, which is what you want.)

2 Cook over medium-low heat for 1 hour, stirring occasionally.

Behind the Recipe:

"My hometown of Huntington, West Virginia, has several famous hot dog drive-ins. The one thing that they're all known for is their hotdogs topped with a meaty red sauce. Boy are they good. The problem is, the recipe for the sauce is a closely guarded secret. So after realizing no one would share this recipe with me, I decided to come up with my own version. This way I can enjoy the taste of back home, while in California, where I reside today. I sometimes serve them like they do in West Virginia, over a steamed hot dog in a toasted or steamed bun, topped off with some crunchy coleslaw...they call those 'slaw dawgs.'"

Jim Thornton, Announcer
4 years at Wheel of Fortune

SMOKEY TEXAS BEEF BRISKET

Serves 8

3 tablespoons smoked paprika, divided

3 tablespoons brown sugar

2 tablespoons chili powder

1 tablespoon ground cumin

2 teaspoons salt

2 teaspoons black pepper

1 (3- to 4-pound) beef brisket

1 cup barbecue sauce

¼ cup water

1 large onion, thinly sliced

1 In a small bowl, combine 2 tablespoons paprika, the brown sugar, chili powder, cumin, salt, and pepper; mix well. Rub mixture evenly over entire surface of brisket. Place in a large resealable plastic bag and refrigerate overnight.

2 In a 6-quart or larger slow cooker, combine barbecue sauce, water, and remaining paprika; mix well. Place brisket over sauce and top with sliced onions. Cover and cook on LOW 8 to 9 hours, or until fork-tender. Let rest 10 minutes, then slice across the grain and serve with the onions and the sauce.

When you see a recipe that says to cut a piece of meat "across the grain," do you know what that means? Meat, just like wood, has grain to it. So once you identify the direction of the grain, it's important to slice the meat across the direction of the grain. That will ensure more tender cuts. If you cut with the grain, the results will be tough and stringy.

MELT-IN-YOUR-MOUTH POT ROAST

Serves 8

- 2 (10.75-ounce) cans condensed cream of mushroom soup
- 1 (1-ounce) package dry onion soup mix
- ¾ cup beef broth
- 1 pound mushrooms, cut in half
- 1 (3- to 4-pound) boneless beef chuck roast
- 1 teaspoon garlic powder
- 1 teaspoon salt
- ½ teaspoon black pepper

1 In a 5-quart or larger slow cooker, combine mushroom soup, soup mix, broth, and mushrooms.

2 Sprinkle roast on all sides with garlic powder, salt, and pepper, and place in slow cooker.

3 Cover and cook on LOW 8 to 10 hours or on HIGH 6 to 7 hours, or until meat is tender. Cut roast into chunks and serve with mushroom gravy.

Test Kitchen Tip: Forgot to thaw your roast? Don't panic! You can cook it from frozen...just make sure you add an additional hour to the cooking time.

Looking Back:

When the show first began (more than 30 years ago), contestants would use their winnings to shop for prizes on the program. One of the most popular choices was a life-size, ceramic Dalmatian named Sheldon. While the shopping format went away in 1987, Sheldon has "lived" on and is now thought of as the official Wheel of Fortune mascot. Back then, Sheldon was priced at $154. Now he's priceless, just like this recipe.

Another thing that is priceless are the photos taken by Carol Kaelson (to the left), the Wheel of Fortune Show Photographer. Thank you, Carol. You make everyone look like a winner!

GARLIC ROASTED PRIME RIB

Serves 6

6 pounds boneless beef prime rib

¼ cup olive oil

1 teaspoon dried thyme

1 teaspoon onion powder

1-¼ teaspoons salt, divided

½ teaspoon black pepper

¼ cup chopped fresh garlic

¼ cup red wine

¼ cup beef broth

1 Preheat oven to 350 degrees F. Coat a roasting pan with cooking spray. Place prime rib, fat side up, on a rack in roasting pan.

2 In a small bowl, combine olive oil, thyme, onion powder, 1 teaspoon salt, the pepper, and garlic; mix well. Rub mixture evenly over entire piece of meat.

3 Roast 30 minutes, then reduce oven to 300 degrees and continue cooking about 2-½ hours for medium-rare, or until meat thermometer reaches 135 degrees, or to desired doneness beyond that. Remove to a cutting board and let rest 15 minutes, tented with aluminum foil, before carving across grain.

4 Meanwhile, on the stovetop over medium heat, add wine, broth, and remaining salt to pan, and whisk 2 to 3 minutes, or until pan is deglazed. (See Tip.) Drizzle pan drippings over sliced prime rib.

Test Kitchen Tip: Before deglazing the pan, make sure it's safe to use on your stove top. If not, place the pan drippings and all the ingredients for the sauce in a sauce pan, and simmer until it reduces slightly.

Behind the Scenes:

Have you ever wondered what it would be like to have Pat or Vanna's job? Well, since they aren't stepping down anytime soon, at least here you can see what it looks like from their perspective. I guess you could say this is a prime example of the perfect job!

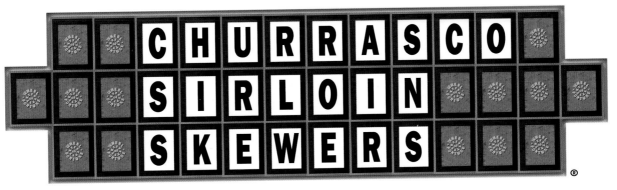
Serves 6

2 cups olive oil

¼ cup fresh lime juice

1 cup fresh parsley, stems removed

8 cloves garlic

1 teaspoon salt

½ teaspoon black pepper

2 pounds boneless top sirloin steak, cut into ½-inch strips

36 (6-inch) skewers

1 In a food processor or blender, combine olive oil, lime juice, parsley, garlic, salt, and pepper; process until well mixed. Reserve ½ cup marinade; cover and set aside until ready to serve.

2 Thread one strip of steak onto each skewer. Place in a 9-x 13-inch baking dish and pour marinade over steak; cover and refrigerate at least 2 hours, or overnight.

3 Heat a grill pan over medium-high heat and cook steak on skewers 2 to 3 minutes per side, or until desired doneness. Serve with reserved marinade.

Test Kitchen Tip: If you'd rather cook these on the grill and you're using bamboo skewers, make sure you soak them in water about 30 minutes before you skewer the meat. That will help prevent them from burning. On the other hand, if you're using metal skewers, you want to be extra careful with them because they will be very hot.

Insider Info:

"I think so many people have worked at Wheel of Fortune for so long because it's the best job in show business! Along with coveted job security, it's a fun gig. Production meetings are filled with humor. If you can't have fun producing a game show where people win cash & prizes, something's wrong! Plus, the meals we eat in the studio and on the road are wheely good! It may sound corny, but it's true."

Brooke Eaton, Producer
15 years at Wheel of Fortune

HAWAIIAN ISLAND ROAST PORK

Serves 8

1 (4- to 5- pound) boneless pork shoulder

1 tablespoon salt

1 teaspoon black pepper

2 teaspoons garlic powder

1 cup pineapple preserves

½ cup jalapeño pepper jelly

½ cup light brown sugar

1 Preheat oven to 300 degrees F. Place pork on a large piece of foil and evenly sprinkle on all sides with salt, pepper, and garlic powder. Seal foil tightly and place in a roasting pan.

2 Roast 3-½ hours, or until meat easily breaks apart with a fork. Carefully unwrap pork and pull apart into chunks; place on a platter.

3 In a small saucepan over low heat, combine pineapple preserves, pepper jelly, and brown sugar. Stir just until sugar is dissolved and serve with pork.

Test Kitchen Tip: Can't find pineapple preserves? No problem. Mango or apricot work great, too!

Did You Know?

One of the crew's favorite spots to tape on location is the Hawaiian Islands. Although it's a lot of work, they like it so much they've been back five times over the years. And when they go, they don't pack lightly. They bring a crew of more than 150 from L.A., and hire an additional 90 to 100 local crew. They also bring approximately 1 million pounds of equipment to tape on the road. And that number doesn't even include their bathing suits and sunscreen!

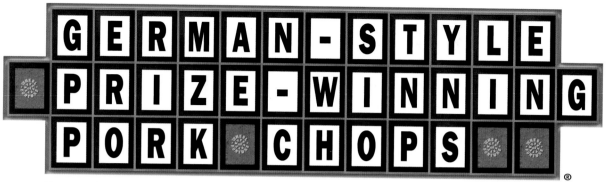

GERMAN-STYLE PRIZE-WINNING PORK CHOPS®

Serves 4

- 4 (½-inch-thick) well-marbled bone-in pork chops
- 1 teaspoon seasoning salt
- 2 tablespoons olive oil
- 1 cup heavy cream
- 2 teaspoons red wine vinegar
- ¼ teaspoon ground nutmeg

1 Season pork chops on both sides with seasoning salt; let sit a few minutes.

2 In a large skillet over medium-high heat, heat oil. Cook pork chops 4 to 6 minutes per side, or until browned. Reduce heat to medium-low.

3 Add cream, vinegar, and nutmeg; stir well. Reduce heat to low and simmer 10 to 12 minutes, or until chops are cooked to medium, or to desired doneness beyond that, and the sauce has thickened, stirring frequently. Serve immediately.

Test Kitchen Tip: If you don't have heavy cream on hand, you can substitute an equal amount of sour cream. It'll still give the sauce a nice creamy texture.

RECIPE CONTEST WINNER

"I grew up in Germany where beef was rather costly, which meant we ate a lot of pork and chicken. A friend of my mother made this once when we were their guests, and I fell in love with it! Years later, when I was just learning how to cook, I remembered how good it was and asked my friend's mom for the recipe. Since then, with a tweak here and there, it has become our quick go-to dinner when there's not a lot of time to fix anything."

Ursula Leach
Culpepper, VA

BBQ PORK TORTILLA STACK

Serves 4

1 (15-ounce) container refrigerated barbecue shredded pork

1 cup frozen corn, thawed

5 (8-inch) flour tortillas

1-½ cups prepared guacamole

2 cups shredded Cheddar cheese, divided

1 Preheat oven to 350 degrees F. Coat a 9-inch round cake pan with cooking spray.

2 In a medium bowl, combine pork and corn; mix well. Place 1 tortilla in cake pan and spread with half the pork mixture; top with another tortilla. Spread with guacamole and top with another tortilla. Sprinkle with 1 cup cheese and top with another tortilla. Spread with remaining pork mixture and top with remaining tortilla.

3 Cover with foil and bake 25 minutes. Uncover and sprinkle with remaining cheese. Bake 5 more minutes, or until cheese is melted. Cut into wedges and serve.

Serving Suggestion: Finish these off with a dollop of sour cream and some guacamole and dig in. Yummy!

If you're looking for a tasty, change-of-pace recipe to throw together before watching Wheel, this is it. As a matter of fact, you can assemble this the night before and simply bake it off right before dinner. And with only one pan to wash, you'll be cleaned up before the first Toss-Up Round.

GAME-CHANGING PORK MARSALA

Serves 4

- 2 tablespoons flour
- ½ teaspoon salt
- ⅛ teaspoon black pepper
- 1 (14- to 16-ounce) pork tenderloin
- 3 tablespoons olive oil
- ½ pound mushrooms, sliced
- 1 onion, cut in half and thinly sliced
- ½ cup sweet Marsala wine

1 In a shallow dish, combine flour, salt, and pepper; mix well. Coat tenderloin with mixture.

2 In a large skillet or Dutch oven over medium-high heat, heat oil until hot, but not smoking. Sear tenderloin 6 to 8 minutes, turning to brown on all sides; remove to a platter and set aside. Add mushrooms and onion to skillet and sauté 6 to 8 minutes, or until tender, stirring occasionally; stir in wine.

3 Return tenderloin to skillet and cook 6 to 8 minutes for medium, or until desired doneness. Slice tenderloin and serve topped with mushrooms and Marsala sauce.

Did You Know?

The USDA now suggests that pork roasts (not ground pork) can safely be cooked to an internal temperature of 145 degrees F. In most cases, this will result in a pork roast that is pinker on the inside than most of us are used to. Following these new recommendations will help make one of America's favorite meats even more flavorful and juicy.

TROPICAL SWEET 'N' SOUR SPARERIBS

Serves 4

½ cup soy sauce

½ cup flour

2 tablespoons vegetable oil

3 to 4 pounds pork spareribs, cut into individual ribs

1-½ cups white vinegar

1-½ cups pineapple juice

1-½ cups water

1-½ cups sugar

1 (20-ounce) can pineapple tidbits, juice reserved

1 red or green bell pepper, chopped

1 In a medium bowl, combine soy sauce with flour to make a paste; set aside.

2 In a large pot or deep skillet over high heat, heat oil; cook ribs in batches 3 to 4 minutes per side, or until browned. Remove ribs to a baking sheet, repeating until all ribs are browned. Coat ribs evenly on all sides with soy paste, reserving any extra. Return to pot and cook in batches 3 to 4 minutes more per side, or until brown and crispy; remove to a baking sheet. Drain excess fat.

3 Add vinegar, pineapple juice, water, and sugar to pot and cook 3 to 5 minutes, or until sugar is dissolved. Stir in remaining flour mixture.

4 Return ribs to pot and heat until mixture starts to boil. Cover, reduce heat to low, and simmer 1 hour, or until tender. Add pineapple and bell pepper and cook 10 minutes. Spoon the sauce over the ribs and enjoy.

RECIPE CONTEST WINNER

"I was born and raised in Hawaii, however these Tropical Sweet 'n' Sour Spareribs were originally shared with me by a friend from California. Over the years, with a few personal touches, they've become one of my family's favorites. This dish is even more delicious as a leftover, and also freezes well."

Pamela Barrineau Williams
Laurel, MS

Vanna Over The Years

Did you know that Vanna never wears the same thing twice on
Wheel of Fortune? That means that over the years, she's graced America with
over 6000 beautiful outfits. Every few weeks, 50 to 60 loaner outfits are
brought in for her to select from. After each taping, they are either sent back
or occasionally auctioned off for charity. Can you put the above photos in
chronological order, starting with the earliest one? (Answers on p. 224.)

Sensational Seafood & Pasta

TROPICAL GETAWAY FRIED SHRIMP

Serves 4

¾ cup mango jelly

1 tablespoon finely chopped fresh jalapeño

1 tablespoon lemon juice

⅛ teaspoon plus ½ teaspoon salt, divided

¾ cup self-rising flour

½ teaspoon cayenne pepper

2 eggs

¼ cup coconut milk

¾ cup vegetable oil

1 pound extra large shrimp, peeled and deveined, with tails left on

1 In a small bowl, combine jelly, jalapeño, lemon juice, and ⅛ teaspoon salt; mix well and set aside.

2 In a shallow dish, combine flour, the remaining salt, and the cayenne pepper; mix well. In another shallow dish, whisk eggs and coconut milk until well combined.

3 In a large skillet over medium-high heat, heat oil until hot but not smoking.

4 Dip shrimp in flour mixture then egg mixture and again in flour mixture, coating completely. Place in skillet and cook 1 to 2 minutes per side, or until coating is golden. Drain on a paper towel-lined platter. Serve immediately with mango sauce.

Serving Suggestion: For a more tropical flavor, sprinkle with toasted coconut before serving.

Always Exciting!

No matter how many times we've watched it, it's always exciting when at the end of the Prize Puzzle Round, Pat turns to the contestant and tells them they've won a trip...often to someplace tropical. You name an island or some sandy beach, and Wheel of Fortune has probably given away a trip to it. And for you at home, it's easy to be a winner with this recipe. You don't even have to leave the house to take your taste buds on their own tropical adventure.

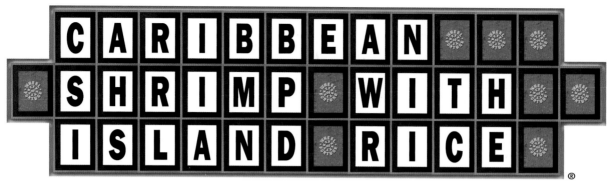

CARIBBEAN SHRIMP WITH ISLAND RICE®

Serves 4

3 cups warm cooked rice

1 (8-ounce) can pineapple tidbits, drained, with ¼ cup juice reserved

1 tablespoon sugar

1 teaspoon salt, divided

2 tablespoons chopped fresh cilantro, divided

1 stick butter

1 tablespoon olive oil

1 pound extra large shrimp, peeled and deveined

3 tablespoons lime juice

1-½ teaspoons chili powder

1 In a medium bowl, combine rice, pineapple (without the reserved juice), the sugar, ½ teaspoon salt, and 1 tablespoon cilantro; mix well, cover, and keep warm.

2 In a large skillet over medium heat, heat butter and oil; sauté shrimp 2 minutes, turning once. Stir in lime juice, chili powder, the reserved pineapple juice, the remaining salt, and the remaining cilantro; heat 1 to 2 minutes, or until shrimp are pink.

3 Spoon shrimp mixture over rice mixture and serve immediately.

Did You Know?
Pat and Vanna really do visit many of the destinations featured in the prizes awarded on the show. It may look like all fun and games, but all that traveling and then shooting promos in the hot sun is no easy task. OK, there are probably worse jobs out there.

MILLION DOLLAR CRAB CAKES®

Makes 10 crab cakes

½ cup mayonnaise

1 egg

1 tablespoon Dijon mustard

2 cloves garlic, minced

2 teaspoons seafood seasoning

¼ teaspoon salt

¼ teaspoon black pepper

¾ cup bread crumbs

1 pound lump crabmeat

4 tablespoons olive oil

1 In a large bowl, whisk together mayonnaise, egg, mustard, garlic, seafood seasoning, salt, and pepper. After it is well mixed, gently stir in bread crumbs and crabmeat until just combined. Do not over mix. Form mixture into 10 crab cakes and place on a platter.

2 In a large skillet over medium heat, heat 2 tablespoons oil. Sauté crab cakes 4 to 6 minutes per side, or until golden brown. Remove to a platter and cover with foil to keep warm. Repeat with remaining crab cakes, adding oil as needed.

Did You Know?

These Maryland-style crab cakes aren't the only thing that Maryland is known for these days. It's also the home of Sarah Manchester, who was the third million dollar winner on Wheel of Fortune. The puzzle she solved was "LOUD LAUGHTER" and that, along with shrieks of joy, were heard after Pat showed her what she had just won. (See recipe photo on page 119.)

WEEKNIGHT FISH & CHIP TACOS

Makes 6

1 (11.4-ounce) package frozen fish sticks

6 (6-inch) flour tortillas

3 cups coleslaw mix

½ cup coleslaw dressing

1 cup coarsely crushed salt and vinegar potato chips

1 Bake fish sticks according to package directions. During the last 5 minutes of cooking, wrap the tortillas in foil and place in the oven to warm through.

2 Meanwhile, in a medium bowl, combine coleslaw mix and dressing. Stir until well combined.

3 Evenly divide fish sticks down center of each tortilla. Top with coleslaw and potato chips. Fold up tortillas (as shown below) and serve.

Test Kitchen. Mr. Food Hints & Tips

This has to be one of the easiest recipes ever. When you first look at the recipe, you might think, "Are the potato chips really supposed to go right on top of each taco?" Well, the answer is yes! The salt-and-vinegar chips add a crispy crunch to each bite and give the tacos a bit of an English flair—traditionally, fish and chips are served with malt vinegar. Yum!

VANNA'S LEMON-CAPER FISH FILLETS

Serves 4

- 3 tablespoons fresh lemon juice
- 2 tablespoons olive oil
- 1 tablespoon finely chopped shallots
- 1 tablespoon capers
- ¼ teaspoon salt, divided
- ¼ teaspoon black pepper, divided
- 4 (6-ounce) white-fleshed fish fillets (like cod or haddock)
- 1 tablespoon chopped chives

1 In a small bowl, whisk together lemon juice, oil, shallot, capers, ⅛ teaspoon salt, and ⅛ teaspoon pepper; set aside.

2 Heat a nonstick grill pan or skillet over medium-high heat. Coat pan with cooking spray. Sprinkle fish with remaining salt and pepper.

3 Place fish in pan and grill 4 minutes per side, or until fish flakes easily with a fork. Spoon sauce over fish, sprinkle with chives, and serve.

Behind the Recipe:

Growing up in North Myrtle Beach, SC, Vanna enjoyed her fair share of seafood. Even though she moved to L.A. to pursue her modeling career in 1980 (before landing her gig on Wheel of Fortune), she never lost her love of seafood. That was obvious when she shared this quick weeknight-friendly skillet dinner that's one of her family's favorites.

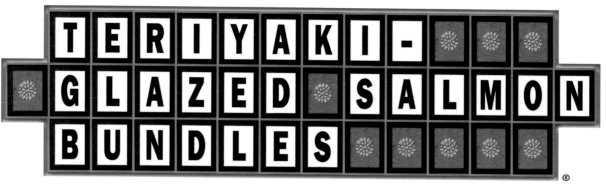

TERIYAKI-GLAZED SALMON BUNDLES

Serves 4

4 (4-ounce) salmon fillets

¼ teaspoon ground ginger

¼ teaspoon garlic powder

¼ teaspoon salt

¼ teaspoon black pepper

4 scallions

1 tablespoon sesame oil

¼ cup teriyaki sauce

2 teaspoons light brown sugar

Sesame seeds for sprinkling

1 Preheat oven to 375 degrees F. Place 4 pieces of aluminum foil, each about 8 inches long, on the counter. Place a salmon fillet on each piece of foil.

2 In a small bowl, combine ginger, garlic, salt, and pepper; mix well. Evenly sprinkle seasoning mixture over salmon, top with a scallion, and drizzle with sesame oil. Fold up foil, making sure seams are sealed. Place on baking sheet. Bake 15 to 20 minutes, or until fish flakes easily with a fork.

3 Meanwhile, in a small bowl, combine teriyaki sauce and brown sugar to make a glaze; mix well. Open foil packets carefully (they will be very hot inside), drizzle with glaze, and sprinkle with sesame seeds. Serve immediately.

Behind the Recipe:

As a loyal Wheel watcher, you know that Wheel of Fortune likes to salute as many cities as possible from all across the country. And you probably know that when the show visits each city, it loves to highlight many of the local sites and foods. After visiting Pike Place Market in Seattle, and watching the fish peddlers toss fresh salmon to one another, it was obvious that a salmon dish belonged in this book. This recipe brings the flavors of the Northwest together in one tasty dish. The only word of caution: don't toss the fish at home, go to Pike Place Market and watch the pros! (See recipe photo on page 119.)

SEAFOOD-CROWNED FISH FILLETS®

Serves 4

- ½ pound imitation crabmeat, flaked
- ½ cup finely crushed saltine crackers
- 1 celery stalk, finely chopped
- 3 tablespoons mayonnaise
- 2 teaspoons lemon juice
- ½ teaspoon onion powder
- ½ teaspoon black pepper
- 1-½ pounds white-fleshed fish fillets (4 pieces)
- ¼ stick butter, melted
- ¼ teaspoon paprika

1 Preheat oven to 375 degrees F. Coat a baking sheet with cooking spray.

2 In a medium bowl, combine crabmeat, cracker crumbs, celery, mayonnaise, lemon juice, onion powder, and pepper; mix well.

3 Place fish fillets on baking sheet. Spoon crabmeat mixture evenly over each fillet. Drizzle with melted butter and sprinkle with paprika.

4 Bake 25 to 30 minutes, or until fish flakes easily with a fork. Serve immediately.

Insider Info:

If you love watching Wheel of Fortune on TV, imagine how fun it would be to watch it being taped live at the Sony Pictures Studios in Culver City, California? To get free tickets, just go online to www.wheeloffortune.com for more information. Once you walk through the studio doors, it will be an experience you'll never forget!

MARDI GRAS JAMBALAYA

Serves 6

- 1 tablespoon olive oil
- 2 green bell peppers, coarsely chopped
- 1 large onion, coarsely chopped
- 4 cups chicken broth
- 2 (15-ounce) cans diced tomatoes, undrained
- 1 cup uncooked white rice
- 2 cloves garlic, minced
- 1 tablespoon Creole seasoning
- ½ pound boneless, skinless chicken breasts, cut into 1-inch chunks
- 1 pound andouille sausage, cut into 1-inch slices
- ½ pound large shrimp, peeled and deveined

1 In a soup pot over medium-high heat, heat oil. Add peppers and onion and sauté 5 to 6 minutes, or until softened.

2 Stir in broth, tomatoes, rice, garlic, and Creole seasoning. Bring to a boil, then cover and reduce heat to medium-low. Cook 20 minutes.

3 Stir in chicken and sausage and cook 5 minutes. Add shrimp and cook 3 to 5 minutes, or until shrimp are pink. Serve immediately.

When you're stuffed from a big bowl of jambalaya, loosen your belt, put on a pot of chicory coffee, and get ready for dessert because no Cajun meal is complete without some beignets. See page 212 for an easy and tasty recipe.

"I've had 12 years of good times traveling the country with the Wheelmobile family and we keep rolling.

I'm very grateful and fortunate to travel the country working for America's Game®. The best part of my job is meeting and talking to the enthusiastic Wheel Watchers as we travel from city to city. I can feel their love and passion for the show, as well as their love for their cities.

Every city is passionate about food, but New Orleans takes it up a notch. This is a city that celebrates its food, music, people, and the Saints. Who dat? The passion pours out of them during the contestant interviews on the Wheelmobile stage. This is where I get a chance to experience the city and its food through their eyes. 'Marty you have to try the gumbo here, the jambalaya here, the Po' Boys here, and on and on.' At the end of a Wheelmobile event, I can't wait to eat and eat and eat some more. And when the Wheelmobile comes to your town, make sure you come by and say hello. We'd love to meet you."

Marty Lublin
Traveling Road Host of the Wheelmobile
12 years at Wheel of Fortune

See more Wheelmobile images and fun facts, on page xxii. If you would like to know when the Wheelmobile is coming to your town, watch for announcements on your local Wheel station, or sign up for Wheel news on www.wheeloffortune.com.

CHICKEN ALFREDO BAKED ZITI ®

Serves 6

1 pound ziti pasta

2 (15-ounce) jars Alfredo sauce

3 cups shredded cooked chicken

2 cups fresh broccoli florets, cut into bite-sized pieces

½ cup thinly sliced sundried tomatoes

1 teaspoon garlic powder

½ teaspoon salt

½ teaspoon black pepper

1-½ cups shredded mozzarella cheese

1 Preheat oven to 350 degrees F. Coat a 3-quart baking dish with cooking spray.

2 In a large pot, cook ziti according to package directions; drain and return to pot. Add Alfredo sauce, chicken, broccoli, sundried tomatoes, garlic powder, salt, and pepper; mix until evenly coated.

3 Pour half the pasta mixture into baking dish, sprinkle with 1 cup mozzarella cheese, add remaining pasta mixture, and sprinkle with remaining cheese. Cover with aluminum foil.

4 Bake 40 minutes, then remove foil and bake an additional 10 to 15 minutes, or until heated through.

Insider Info:
When Pat gives the Wheel a final spin, if, by chance, he lands on the Bankrupt wedge, it gets edited out during post production and he spins again. And all these years you thought Pat knew some secret about how to avoid that dreaded wedge!

OLD WORLD POLISH-STYLE LASAGNA

Serves 9

- 9 lasagna noodles, cooked al dente
- 1 (24-ounce) container small curd cottage cheese
- 1 egg
- 1 (16-ounce) can sauerkraut, well drained
- 3 cups mashed potatoes
- ¼ cup chopped onion, sautéed
- 1 (8-ounce) block Cheddar cheese, shredded, divided
- ¼ cup melted butter

1 Preheat oven to 350 degrees F. Coat a 9- x 13-inch baking dish with cooking spray. Place 3 noodles in bottom.

2 In a small bowl, mix cottage cheese and egg. Spread over noodles in baking dish.

3 Place 3 noodles over cottage cheese layer. Spread sauerkraut over second layer of noodles. Place remaining noodles over sauerkraut.

4 In a medium bowl, combine potatoes, onion, and ½ the shredded cheese. Spread over noodles, top with remaining cheese, and drizzle with melted butter.

5 Cover with aluminum foil and bake 30 minutes. Remove foil and continue to bake 30 additional minutes, or until heated in center. Let stand 10 minutes before serving.

Test Kitchen Tip: If you prefer to use whole wheat lasagna noodles, go ahead. It'll be just as good either way!

RECIPE CONTEST WINNER

"This is one of my favorite comfort foods. If there are any leftovers (which rarely happens since this is so good), refrigerate them and reheat them in the microwave for about 2 minutes, leaving you plenty of time to get cozy for watching Wheel of Fortune."

Sue Cullen
Stetsonville, WI

WORTH THE WAIT LASAGNA

Serves 9

12 lasagna noodles

1 pound bulk hot Italian sausage

4 cups shredded mozzarella cheese, divided

1 (15-ounce) container ricotta cheese

⅓ cup grated Parmesan cheese

1 egg

½ teaspoon dried basil

½ teaspoon black pepper

2 (28-ounce) jars spaghetti sauce

1 Preheat oven to 375 degrees F. Coat a 9- x 13-inch baking dish with cooking spray. Cook lasagna noodles according to package directions; drain.

2 Meanwhile, in a large skillet over medium-high heat, cook sausage until no pink remains, stirring to break up sausage as it cooks. Drain off excess liquid and set aside in a large bowl to cool slightly. Add 3 cups mozzarella cheese, the ricotta and Parmesan cheeses, the egg, basil, and pepper; mix well.

3 Spread 1 cup spaghetti sauce over bottom of baking dish. Place 3 noodles over sauce. Spread one-third of sausage mixture over noodles. Pour 1 cup spaghetti sauce over sausage mixture. Place 3 more noodles over the top and press down lightly. Repeat with 2 more layers of sausage mixture, sauce, and noodles. Spoon remaining sauce over top and cover tightly with aluminum foil.

4 Bake 1 hour. Remove foil and sprinkle remaining mozzarella cheese over top; return to oven 5 more minutes, or until cheese has melted. Allow to sit 10 to 15 minutes before cutting and serving.

Behind the Recipe:

If this recipe looks familiar to you, it's because it was one of five international favorites that were part of a recent Fabulous Food week on Wheel of Fortune. All that week, Howard got to make a dish to represent the destination of the trips that were being given away each day. It was so good the crew raced backstage after the taping to try some. Apparently, this lasagna was worth the wait!

WHEELY GOOD MAC & CHEESE

Serves 6

1 pound wagon wheel-shaped pasta

½ stick butter, plus 1 tablespoon butter melted, divided

2 tablespoons flour

1 teaspoon salt

½ teaspoon black pepper

3 cups milk

3 cups shredded sharp Cheddar cheese

2 cups shredded Gouda cheese

¾ cup coarsely crushed butter crackers

1 Preheat oven to 350 degrees F. Coat a 2-½-quart casserole dish with cooking spray.

2 In a soup pot, cook pasta according to package directions; drain and set aside.

3 In the same pot over medium heat, melt the ½ stick butter. Add flour, salt, and pepper; stir to mix well and let cook one minute, stirring constantly. Gradually whisk in milk; bring to a boil and cook until thickened, stirring constantly. Stir in the cheeses and cook until melted. Return pasta to pot; mix well. Spoon mixture into casserole dish.

4 In a small bowl, combine crackers and the 1 tablespoon melted butter. Sprinkle over macaroni and cheese. Bake uncovered 35 to 40 minutes, or until golden and bubbly.

Test Kitchen. Mr. Food Hints & Tips

Is there a more comforting dish to sit down with while watching Wheel of Fortune than mac & cheese? You don't have to think about it. The answer is no. Now, there are lots of shortcut versions around, and they all have their place, but nothing is as good (and we mean wheely good) as our from-scratch, easy-to-throw-together version. And if you happen to have another shape of pasta on hand that you'd rather use, go ahead. There are no rules—either way it's delicious.

SHORTCUT MACARONI & BEEF

Serves 6

1-½ pounds ground beef

1 green bell pepper, chopped

½ cup chopped onion

1 (26-ounce) jar spaghetti sauce

1 teaspoon salt

½ teaspoon black pepper

12 ounces uncooked elbow macaroni

1 cup water

1 cup (4 ounces) shredded mozzarella cheese

1 Preheat oven to 350 degrees F. Coat a 2-½-quart casserole dish with cooking spray.

2 In a large skillet over medium-high heat, brown ground beef, bell pepper, and onion 6 to 8 minutes, or until no pink remains in the beef, stirring frequently. Drain off excess liquid. Add remaining ingredients except cheese; mix well. Place in casserole dish.

3 Cover tightly and bake 30 minutes. Remove from oven, stir, replace cover, and return to oven to bake 20 additional minutes, or until pasta is tender. Remove cover, sprinkle with cheese and bake 5 more minutes, or until cheese is melted.

Test Kitchen. Mr. Food Hints & Tips

The best thing about this dish is that you don't have to cook the pasta separately. It cooks along with everything else, which mean less pots to wash. Ahhh, if only solving tonight's Bonus Round was this easy. Here's hoping it is!

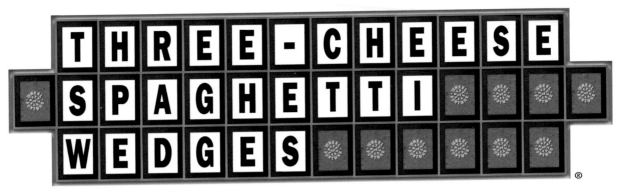

THREE-CHEESE SPAGHETTI WEDGES

Serves 8

1 pound spaghetti

3 eggs

1 cup milk

1 teaspoon garlic powder

1-½ teaspoons salt

½ teaspoon black pepper

1 cup ricotta cheese

½ cup grated Parmesan cheese

2 cups shredded mozzarella cheese, divided

1 Preheat oven to 400 degrees F. Coat a 9-inch springform pan with cooking spray. Cook pasta according to package directions; drain well.

2 In a large bowl, whisk eggs, milk, garlic powder, salt, and pepper. Add ricotta cheese, Parmesan cheese, 1-½ cups mozzarella cheese, and spaghetti; mix well. Pour into pan and press down lightly. Sprinkle with remaining cheese.

3 Bake 40 to 45 minutes, or until the top is golden brown and the center is set. Let cool 10 minutes before removing from pan. Cut into wedges and serve.

Serving Suggestion:

Although this may look more like a piece of cake than a main dish, don't let it fool you— because this is definitely main-dish perfect. And when it comes to serving it, don't even think of topping it with whipped cream! Try spooning on either a rich marinara or pesto sauce. Maybe put out bowls of each so everybody can do their own thing? Decisions, decisions.

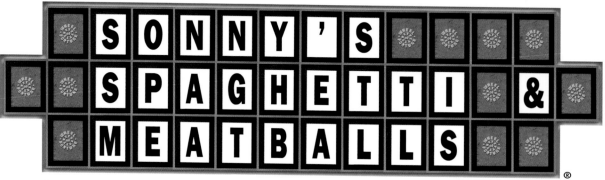

SONNY'S SPAGHETTI & MEATBALLS

Serves 6

½ pound ground pork

½ pound ground beef

¾ cup Italian bread crumbs

½ cup grated Parmesan cheese

½ cup water

¼ cup coarsely chopped fresh parsley

1 egg

1-½ teaspoons garlic powder

1 teaspoon salt

1 teaspoon black pepper

2 (26-ounce) jars spaghetti sauce

1 pound spaghetti

1 In a large bowl, gently combine all ingredients except sauce and spaghetti. Don't overmix, as the meatballs will get tough. Form into 12 meatballs and place in a large pot. Add sauce and stir gently to mix.

2 Bring to a boil over medium heat, then reduce heat to low, cover loosely, and simmer 25 to 30 minutes, or until meatballs are cooked through.

3 Meanwhile, cook spaghetti according to package directions; drain and place on a large serving platter. Spoon sauce and meatballs over spaghetti and serve.

Serving Suggestion: To add a real Mama Mia touch to these, don't forget to grate on some Parmesan cheese. It's like a cherry on a sundae.

Behind the Scenes:

"I have worked at Wheel of Fortune since 2004. Let me tell you I have the best job in the world. Being an Audience Coordinator, I'm the guy who holds up the "APPLAUSE" sign so the audience knows when to clap and the "SHHHH, QUIET, PLEASE!" sign to remind the audience not to shout out what the puzzle is once they figure it out.
At home, I'm the one who does most of the cooking, and the one dish that my family always requests is my applause-worthy spaghetti and meatballs. I hope your family loves this dish as much as mine does. It might even earn you a standing ovation!"

Sonny Goodman, Audience Coordinator
11 years at Wheel of Fortune

SUZY'S FILL-YA-UP GNOCCHI

Serves 4

1 (10-ounce) package gnocchi

3 tablespoons olive oil

3 tablespoons butter

1 (8-ounce) package fresh mushrooms, sliced

1-½ cups frozen peas

2 cloves garlic, minced

½ teaspoon salt

¼ teaspoon black pepper

¾ cup chicken broth

Parmesan cheese for sprinkling

1 Cook gnocchi according to package directions; drain well.

2 Meanwhile, in a large skillet over medium heat, heat oil and melt butter. Add mushrooms, peas, garlic, salt, and pepper; cook 6 to 8 minutes, or until vegetables are tender. Add broth and gnocchi to vegetables and heat 5 to 7 minutes, or until heated through and broth begins to thicken up.

3 Sprinkle with Parmesan cheese and serve.

Test Kitchen Tip: If you're feeling like you want to be super healthy, leave out the butter and the salt, and add in a splash more of olive oil. Either way, it's downright satisfying.

Behind the Recipe:

"After working at Wheel of Fortune for 28 years, do I ever have stories! When I started, I worked with Merv Griffin, the creator of Wheel of Fortune. As you can imagine, I could've never stayed here this long

unless I not only loved what I do but loved the people I work with. Everyone at the show is like family to me. And since many of us have worked together for so long, we all know each other's ways. As for me, I'm an exercise nut and try to eat healthy. This is one of my favorite weeknight meals since it's super fast, loaded with veggies, and there's usually enough left over that I can bring some in to work the next day to share."

Suzy Rosenberg
Publicity & Promotions Producer
28 years at Wheel of Fortune

Great Go-Alongs

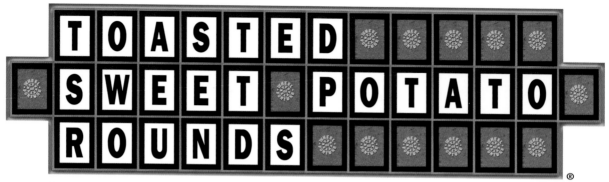

TOASTED SWEET POTATO ROUNDS

Serves 6

- 2 tablespoons vegetable oil
- ½ teaspoon salt
- 2 large unpeeled sweet potatoes, with ends trimmed, cut into ½-inch slices
- ¼ cup light brown sugar
- 3 tablespoons butter, melted
- 2 cups mini marshmallows

1 Preheat oven to 400 degrees F.

2 In a large bowl, combine oil and salt; mix well. Add sweet potato slices and toss until evenly coated. Place on rimmed baking sheet.

3 Bake 15 to 20 minutes, or until fork-tender. Sprinkle each slice with 1 teaspoon brown sugar. Drizzle butter evenly over brown sugar and place marshmallows on top of each slice.

4 Increase oven temperature to broil and broil 1 to 2 minutes, or until marshmallows are lightly toasted. Serve immediately.

Behind the Scenes:

Patty Rosenthal has headed up recipe development for the Mr. Food Test Kitchen for more than 20 years. Her passion for food and attention to detail has earned her recognition with the many companies that she

has created recipes for during her tenure. Since every recipe is triple-tested, you can feel confident of the outcome when you're making these in your kitchen. Besides her love of cooking, Patty is a real dog lover, and you can bet her pride and joy, Truffles, is the best fed (and loved) dog in town. Almost every evening, you can find Patty, her husband, and Truffles unwinding while watching Wheel of Fortune after a busy day of testing, tasting and retesting.

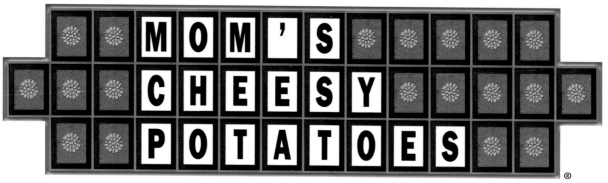

MOM'S CHEESY POTATOES

Serves 6

1 (30-ounce) bag frozen shredded hash brown potatoes, thawed

2 cups shredded sharp Cheddar cheese

1 (10-¾-ounce) can cream of chicken soup

½ cup sour cream

½ teaspoon salt

½ teaspoon black pepper

½ cup Parmesan cheese

1 Preheat oven to 350 degrees F. Coat a 9-inch square or 2-quart baking dish with cooking spray.

2 In a large bowl, combine all ingredients except Parmesan cheese. Pour into baking dish and cover with aluminum foil.

3 Bake 1 hour. Uncover, sprinkle with Parmesan cheese, and bake uncovered another 45 minutes, or until the top is golden.

Behind the Recipe:

"My mom, Gloria, started making these a while back, and, ever since the first bite, my brother and I have requested these any time we are in town or having a holiday meal."

Gina Freeman
Assistant to Supervising Producer
19 years at Wheel of Fortune

PUB-STYLE POTATO WEDGES

Serves 6

¼ cup vegetable oil

1 teaspoon paprika

¼ teaspoon black pepper

3 large Russett potatoes, washed and cut lengthwise into ½-inch wedges

⅓ cup ketchup

1 tablespoon yellow mustard

½ teaspoon salt

1 Preheat oven to 425 degrees F. In a large bowl, combine oil, paprika, and pepper. Add potato wedges and toss until evenly coated. Arrange on baking sheet.

2 Bake 30 minutes. Turn potatoes over and continue cooking 25 to 30 additional minutes, or until golden and crispy.

3 Meanwhile, in a small bowl, make dipping sauce by combining ketchup and mustard; mix well. Sprinkle potatoes with salt and serve with dipping sauce.

Sometimes the simplest recipes are the best ones. And one lesson the Test Kitchen has learned over time is if you start any recipe with great ingredients, you'll end up with great results. That's why, in this recipe, it's best to use only Russett potatoes. The days of thinking that all potatoes are equal are over.

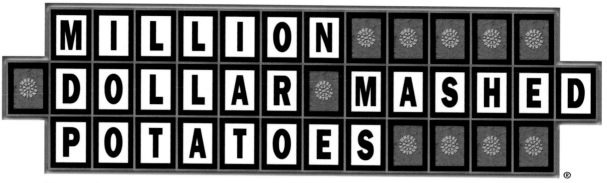

MILLION DOLLAR MASHED POTATOES

Serves 6

3 pounds potatoes, peeled and cut into chunks

6 tablespoons butter

2 tablespoons milk

½ cup ranch dressing

1 teaspoon salt

¼ teaspoon black pepper

1. Place potatoes in a soup pot and add enough water to cover. Bring to a boil over high heat and cook 20 to 25 minutes, or until tender. Drain well and return potatoes to pot. Place pot back on heat for 1 minute or until all the water evaporates.

2. Add remaining ingredients and beat with an electric mixer until smooth and creamy. Serve immediately.

Behind the Recipe:

Picture this: the music is playing, the clock is ticking, the audience is holding its breath... (You know how exciting the Bonus Round is!) Now, imagine what winning big during that round would feel like! For Autumn Erhard, one of the lucky and talented million-dollar winners, it was quite a thrill. "For three and a half months, my parents, fiancé (now husband), and I kept my winnings a secret from everyone. On the drive home from my episode's taping, we all agreed to tell the same story to anyone who asked how I did. We came up with, 'She did well, but she could have done better — I think her nerves got the best of her.' The hardest part was trying to contain our excitement when we had to pick up our puppy from my husband's parents' house that same night. We must have done a good job with misleading everybody, as they were completely shocked when my episode aired."

Autumn Erhard, Million Dollar Winner
Laguna Niguel, CA

FRENCH ONION STUFFED BAKED POTATOES

Serves 4

4 large Russett potatoes, washed

1 tablespoon vegetable oil

1 sweet onion, cut into ¼-inch slivers

2 tablespoons butter

¼ cup beef broth

1 teaspoon salt

½ teaspoon black pepper

4 slices Swiss cheese

1 Preheat oven to 400 degrees F. Pierce top of potatoes several times with a fork and place on a baking sheet. Bake 1 hour, or until fork-tender. Let cool 5 to 10 minutes, or until you can handle them.

2 Meanwhile, in a skillet over medium-high heat, heat oil; sauté onion 12 to 15 minutes, or until golden brown, stirring occasionally.

3 Slice ½ inch off the top of each potato and scoop out pulp, leaving about ¼-inch thick potato shell; place pulp in bowl. Add butter, broth, salt, and pepper; beat until smooth. Stir in onion. Spoon mixture into potato shells.

4 Bake 20 to 25 minutes, or until heated through. Place a slice of cheese on top of each potato and bake an additional 5 minutes, or until cheese is melted. Serve immediately.

If you want, you can make these in advance and freeze them right after you stuff them. When you want them, simply thaw them overnight in the fridge and bake them as suggested above. This is great if you just want 2 when you make 'em and the rest whenever you get the craving, which could be pretty often, considering how good these are.

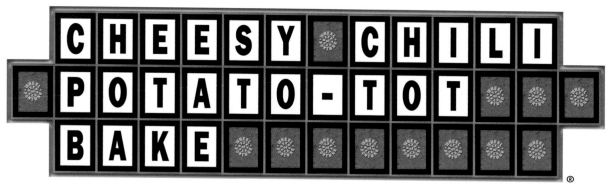

CHEESY CHILI POTATO-TOT BAKE

Serves 8

1 (32-ounce) package frozen potato tots

2 (15-ounce) cans chili

¼ cup chopped red onion

1 cup shredded Cheddar cheese

1 Preheat oven to 425 degrees F. Coat a 9- x 13-inch baking dish with cooking spray. Place potato tots in baking dish. Bake 30 to 35 minutes, or until crispy.

2 Meanwhile, in a microwaveable bowl, warm chili. Evenly spoon over potato tots, then sprinkle with onion and cheese. Return to oven 5 minutes, or until cheese is melted. Serve immediately.

Test Kitchen, Mr. Food Hints & Tips

This is one of those recipes that's easy to make your own by adding any of your family's favorite ingredients. If they like spice, add some chopped jalapeños. Wanna hearty it up even more? Add some diced cooked chicken. You can even make these in individual crocks so everyone gets their very own. How fun is that?

COUNTRY CORNBREAD DRESSING®

Serves 8

1 stick butter

½ cup chopped onion

½ cup chopped celery

4 cornbread muffins

10 slices white bread

1-½ teaspoons poultry seasoning

2 teaspoons sugar

1 teaspoon salt

½ teaspoon black pepper

2 eggs, lightly beaten

1-½ cups chicken stock

½ cup dried cranberries

1 Preheat oven to 350 degrees F. Coat a 1–½-quart baking dish with cooking spray.

2 In a large skillet over medium heat, melt butter; sauté onion and celery 6 to 8 minutes, or until tender.

3 In a food processor, combine muffins and bread, and pulse until coarsely crumbled. Place in a large bowl and add remaining ingredients, including sautéed vegetables; mix well. Place in baking dish and cover with aluminum foil.

4 Bake 30 minutes, uncover, and bake 20 to 25 more minutes, or until heated through.

Insider Info:
The "Wheel! ... Of! ... Fortune!" chant that starts the show was first introduced in the early 1980s. Want to get the official Wheel! Of! Fortune! chant ringtone and other digital downloads? Just visit www.wheeloffortune.com.

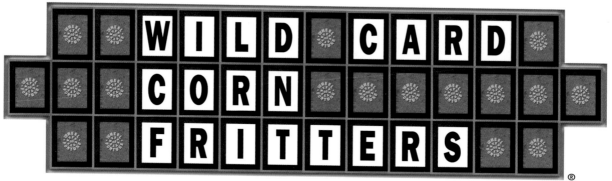

WILD CARD CORN FRITTERS

Makes about 2 dozen fritters

1-¾ cups flour

2 teaspoons baking powder

1-¼ teaspoons salt

½ teaspoon black pepper

2 eggs, beaten

1 (14-¾-ounce) can cream-style corn

1 cup frozen corn, thawed

1 cup shredded pepper jack cheese

¼ cup vegetable oil, plus more if needed

1 In a large bowl, combine flour, baking powder, salt, and pepper. Add eggs; mix well. Stir in both corns and cheese.

2 In a large skillet over medium heat, heat 1 tablespoon oil; drop batter into hot oil 1 tablespoon at a time. Cook 6 to 8 minutes or until golden, turning fritters halfway through cooking. Remove to a covered platter. Repeat with remaining oil and batter until all batter is used.

Did You Know?

If you're lucky and skillful enough to make it to the Bonus Round holding a Wild Card, you'll be able to select an additional consonant, increasing your chances to solve the Bonus Puzzle and win big. That's what inspired us to name these fritters after it.

These are so good, they'll definitely increase your chances of having your kids or grandkids eat their vegetables.

Taping the show must really work up an appetite. So much so, Pat and Vanna will eat just about anything, including a Wild Card. Don't let them fool you—they're actually eating a cookie in the shape of the Wild Card, not the real thing!

BROCCOLI 'N' QUINOA MUFFINS

Makes 12 muffins

- 1 cup quinoa, cooked according to package directions
- 2 cups chopped broccoli
- 2 cups shredded Cheddar cheese
- 2 tablespoons spicy brown mustard
- 3 eggs, lightly beaten
- 1 teaspoon onion powder
- ½ teaspoon salt
- ½ teaspoon black pepper

1 Preheat oven to 350 degrees F. Coat a 12-cup muffin tin with cooking spray.

2 In a large bowl, combine all ingredients; mix well. Spoon mixture evenly into muffin cups.

3 Bake 30 to 35 minutes, or until golden on top. Let sit 5 minutes, remove from pan, and serve.

Test Kitchen.
Mr. Food
Hints & Tips

When something is touted as a super food, it's natural to be a bit skeptical. But the more the Test Kitchen team works with quinoa, the more they like it. After all, it's packed with protein, it's high in fiber, it's gluten-free, and most importantly, it's got a mild taste that makes it quite versatile. As for the super food part—the jury is still out on that one.

"T"-RRIFIC RICE CASSEROLE

Serves 8

- 1-½ cups long-grain rice (uncooked)
- 2 cups sliced fresh mushrooms (about 8 ounces)
- ½ cup chopped onion
- 1-¾ cup chicken broth
- 1 (10-¾-ounce) can condensed cream of mushroom soup
- ½ stick butter, melted
- ½ teaspoon black pepper
- ½ cup French fried onions

1 Preheat oven to 375 degrees F. Coat a 2-quart casserole dish with cooking spray; set aside.

2 In a medium bowl, combine all ingredients except French fried onions; mix well. Spoon mixture into casserole dish.

3 Cover and bake 60 to 65 minutes, or until liquid is absorbed and rice is tender. Sprinkle with French fried onions and serve.

Did You Know?

This side dish is the perfect go-along no matter what you're serving. It's just as at home with chicken as it is with roast pork or even burgers. I guess you could say it fits any meal to a "T". Speaking of "T"s, did you know that "T" was the first letter that Vanna turned when she came to the show in 1982? Oh, by the way, the puzzle was "General Hospital." After all these years, she still looks "T"-rrific!

RED-SKINNED POTATO SALAD

Serves 8

3 pounds red potatoes with skins on, cut into 2-inch chunks

½ cup mayonnaise

½ cup sour cream

1 teaspoon yellow mustard

3 hard-boiled eggs, chopped

2 celery stalks, chopped

2 scallions, thinly sliced

¾ teaspoon salt

½ teaspoon black pepper

1 Place potatoes in a large pot and cover with water. Bring to a boil and cook 15 to 20 minutes, or until fork-tender; drain and cool slightly.

2 In a large bowl, combine remaining ingredients. Add potatoes and toss gently until evenly coated. Cover and chill until ready to serve.

Good For You! Leaving the skins on the potatoes is not only easier, it also ensures we get all the vitamins that are in the skins. It's a double bonus!

Test Kitchen. Mr. Food Hints & Tips

When making potato salad or macaroni salad, we always recommend mixing the dressing while the potatoes or pasta are still warm. This way, the flavor from the dressing is absorbed, making the salad extra yummy. This can be your little secret when everybody asks you what makes your deli salad so good.

FIVE-MINUTE HULA HULA COLESLAW ®

Serves 8

1 (16-ounce) bag coleslaw mix

1-¼ cups mayonnaise

1 (8-ounce) can crushed pineapple, drained

1 (6-ounce) can Mandarin oranges, drained

½ cup shredded coconut, toasted

1 tablespoon sugar

¼ teaspoon salt

¼ teaspoon black pepper

1 In a large bowl, toss together all ingredients until well mixed and evenly coated.

2 Cover and chill until ready to serve. Right before serving, give it a good mix, so all the flavors are well combined.

Serving Suggestion: Want to to go all out when serving this? Serve it out of a pineapple. For that, all you have to do is cut a fresh pineapple in half lengthwise, cut out the flesh, and serve the slaw inside. If you want, you can even dice up some of the pineapple and add it to the slaw to make it extra special.

Behind the Scenes:
What did Pat do during his off time while shooting on location in Hawaii? "When I'm not working, I'm eating," he said and added, "I eat and sit in the sun, and then, I get up and eat some more. Then, I get something to drink. Then, I go to sleep." That must be why he had so much energy, which allowed him to tape 5 shows back-to-back each night they were there.

VANNA'S PINEAPPLE LIME FLUFF®

Serves 12

- 1 (32-ounce) container cottage cheese
- 1 (4-serving size) lime-flavored gelatin mix
- 1 (20-ounce) can crushed pineapple in its own juice, drained
- 1 (8-ounce) container frozen whipped topping, thawed
- 1 cup chopped pecans

1 In a large bowl, place cottage cheese and gelatin mix; mix well. Add pineapple, then fold in whipped topping and pecans.

2 Refrigerate until ready to serve.

Behind the Recipe:

During a recent taping, Howard and Jodi from the Mr. Food Test Kitchen got to visit Vanna in her dressing room between shows. Howard said, "She's such a sweetheart and she greeted us with her Southern hospitality. While chit-chatting about this and that, I asked her what the one dish was that she had at every family get-together when growing up. Well, it didn't take long before she shared with us this Southern classic. Vanna lit up even more than ever as she shared memories of this family treasure."

PARMESAN ROASTED GREEN BEANS

Serves 6

2 tablespoons olive oil

¾ teaspoon dried basil

½ teaspoon garlic powder

¼ teaspoon salt

¼ teaspoon black pepper

1 pound fresh green beans, trimmed

2 tablespoons grated Parmesan cheese

1 Preheat oven to 400 degrees F.

2 In a large bowl, combine olive oil, basil, garlic powder, salt, and pepper. Add green beans and toss until evenly coated. Place on rimmed baking sheet.

3 Roast 25 to 30 minutes, or until tender and browned, turning once halfway through cooking. Sprinkle with Parmesan cheese and serve.

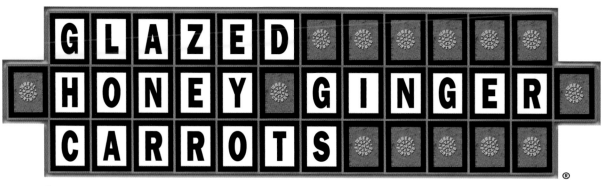

GLAZED HONEY GINGER CARROTS

Serves 6

2 pounds carrots, peeled and cut into 1-inch chunks

1 tablespoon sugar

2 tablespoons butter

1 tablespoon honey

1 teaspoon lemon juice

½ teaspoon ground ginger

¼ teaspoon salt

1 In a medium saucepan, combine carrots and sugar; cover with water. Bring to a boil over high heat, then reduce heat to medium and cook 15 to 20 minutes, or until carrots are fork-tender; drain well and return to pan.

2 Add butter, honey, lemon juice, ginger, and salt to the carrots; mix well. Cook on low 3 to 5 minutes, or until the butter is melted and the sauce starts to thicken.

Test Kitchen Tip: Although at times, the Test Kitchen is a huge fan of the mini pre-peeled carrots, this recipe works much better if you start with whole carrots, peel and cut them, and boil them as directed. The whole carrots are much more tender when cooked.

Fun Fact:

Vanna has her own vegetable garden and throughout the year, she'll bring in some homegrown goodies to share with Pat. Here, she didn't bring in any carrots, but she did bring in zucchini, peaches, and the juiciest tomatoes ever.

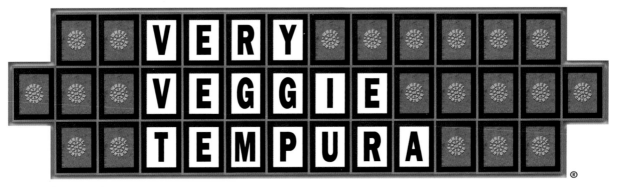

VERY VEGGIE TEMPURA

Serves 6

3 cups vegetable oil

1-¼ cups flour

¾ cup cornstarch, divided

¼ cup baking powder

1 teaspoon garlic powder

1-½ teaspoons salt

⅛ teaspoon cayenne pepper

1-½ cups cold club soda

½ head broccoli, cut into florets

½ pound whole fresh mushrooms

1 zucchini, cut into ½-inch chunks

1 red bell pepper, cut into ¼-inch strips

1 In a soup pot over medium-high heat, heat oil just until hot, but not smoking.

2 In a large bowl, combine flour, ½ cup cornstarch, the baking powder, garlic powder, salt, and cayenne pepper. Add club soda and mix well.

3 Lightly dust vegetables with remaining cornstarch, then dip a few at a time into the batter. Gently place in the hot oil and cook 4 to 5 minutes, or until golden, turning to cook evenly. Remove with a slotted spoon and drain on paper towels. Repeat until all vegetables are cooked.

4 Serve immediately or place on a baking sheet and keep warm in a low oven.

Serving Suggestion:

*To finish this off, whip up a batch of the Test Kitchen's **Garlic Ginger Dipping Sauce** and dip away. To make it, simply whisk together ½ cup soy sauce, ¼ cup rice wine vinegar, 1 teaspoon sesame oil, 2 teaspoons sugar, ¼ teaspoon garlic powder, ⅛ teaspoon ground ginger, and 2 tablespoons thinly sliced scallion.*

Here the camera caught Howard from the Mr. Food Test Kitchen sneaking some Tempura between takes, during Fabulous Food week. No worries, there was no double dipping involved and once you try these, you'll understand just how irresistible they are.

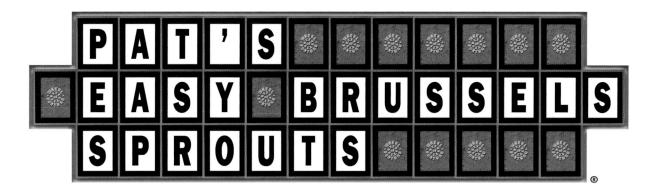

PAT'S EASY BRUSSELS SPROUTS

¼ cup olive oil

½ teaspoon garlic powder

¼ teaspoon onion powder

½ teaspoon salt

¼ teaspoon black pepper

1 pound Brussels sprouts, trimmed and cut in half

4 slices bacon

½ cup chopped onion

½ pound mushrooms, sliced

1 Preheat oven to 425 degrees F.

2 In a large bowl, combine oil, garlic powder, onion powder, salt, and pepper. Add Brussels sprouts and gently toss until evenly coated. Place on rimmed baking sheet. Bake 25 to 30 minutes, or until tender and the edges get crispy, turning once halfway through.

3 Meanwhile, in a large skillet over medium-high heat, cook bacon 8 to 10 minutes, or until crispy, turning once. Remove to a paper towel-lined plate, but reserve bacon drippings in skillet. Let bacon cool, then crumble. Place onion and mushrooms in skillet with bacon drippings and cook over medium heat 5 to 7 minutes, or until tender.

4 In a large bowl, toss the sprouts with mushrooms and onions, sprinkle with bacon, and serve.

Behind the Recipe:

"When host Pat Sajak was describing his love of Brussels sprouts with us during a commercial break on a recent taping day, we could hear the passion in his voice. As he slowly described how he makes them, they sounded so good that I was practically drooling, and my stomach was starting to grumble. At that point, Pat

had to go back and finish taping the Mother's Day shows. Just moments later, during the quiet hush right before the Bonus Round, my stomach seemed to growl as if it was still thinking of his recipe. It seemed so loud to me ... I thought everyone in the studio heard it. Luckily, no one else seemed to notice and since we were sitting just a few feet away from Pat and the big winner of the day, I would have been mortified! (Good thing it was all in my head!)"

Jodi Flayman, Director of Publishing
11 years at Mr. Food Test Kitchen

POTLUCK BUBBLIN' BAKED BEANS

Serves 8

6 slices bacon

1 large onion, coarsely chopped

2 cloves garlic, minced

1 (28-ounce) can baked beans

1 (15-ounce) can small lima beans, drained

1 (15.5-ounce) can kidney beans, drained

½ cup brown sugar

¾ cup ketchup

1 Preheat oven to 350 degrees F.

2 In a medium skillet over high heat, cook bacon until crisp; remove to a paper towel-lined plate. Sauté onion and garlic in pan drippings.

3 In a 9- x 13-inch baking dish, combine remaining ingredients. Crumble bacon and add to mixture. Drain onion and garlic, reserving a small amount of pan drippings. Add onion mixture and reserved pan drippings to baking dish; mix well. Bake 1 hour, or until mixture is heated through.

Test Kitchen Tip: You can also make this in a slow cooker. It'll take about 3 to 4 hours on LOW.

RECIPE CONTEST WINNER

"This is a fantastic dish to take to a potluck since it's easy to make and is just as good even if it's not served piping hot. I've made these for years and, as far as I can remember, my mother began making these back in the 1960's. It's one of those dishes that tastes great, reheats well, and can be doubled or tripled for large get-togethers. And if you want, leave out the bacon to make it vegetarian."

Cynthia Smith
Hammond, IN

A Little Bit of This 'n' That

PAT'S PERFECT PIZZA PIE ®

Makes 1 pizza

- ½ pound Italian sausage, casing removed
- 1-½ cups sliced mushrooms
- ½ cup chopped onion
- 1 pound fresh store-bought pizza dough
- ½ cup pizza sauce
- 1 cup shredded mozzarella cheese
- ½ a jalapeño, thinly sliced and seeded

1 Preheat oven to 450 degrees F. Coat a 12-inch pizza pan with cooking spray.

2 In a skillet over high heat, sauté sausage 6 to 8 minutes, or until no pink remains. Add mushrooms and onion and cook 4 to 5 minutes, or just until vegetables are tender. Drain excess liquid; set aside.

3 Using a rolling pin or your fingers, stretch dough to fit pizza pan. Push dough to the edge of the pan, forming a rim. With a fork, prick dough 10 to 15 times.

4 Spoon sauce evenly over dough and top with cheese. Spoon sausage mixture evenly over cheese and top with jalapeño slices.

5 Bake 15 to 18 minutes, or until crust is crispy and golden brown. Cut into slices and serve.

Behind the Recipe:

"Between rounds of a recent taping, I chatted with Pat about some of his favorite foods. I was surprised when he said that he loves making homemade pizza. He went on to share the details. He likes lots of cheese,

sausage, onions, and mushrooms. When I asked about pepperoni, he said, "Nope, not a fan of pepperoni on pizza." He also said he likes the kick that a sliced jalapeño adds, and he likes to bake it until the crust is really crispy. After that, he turned to me and said, "I better get going, it's time for another Toss-Up round, and they can't start that without me."

Howard Rosenthal
On-Air Personality/Chief Food Officer
21 years at Mr. Food Test Kitchen

MEAT LOVER'S CHICAGO DEEP-DISH PIZZA ®

Makes 1 pizza

¾ pound hot Italian sausage, casing removed

1 green bell pepper, chopped

1 small onion, chopped

1 pound fresh store-bought pizza dough

½ cup spaghetti sauce

12 slices pepperoni

1 cup shredded mozzarella cheese

1 Preheat oven to 450 degrees F. Coat a 10-inch springform pan with cooking spray.

2 In a large skillet over medium heat, cook sausage, pepper, and onion 6 to 8 minutes, or until no pink remains in the sausage and vegetables are tender, stirring constantly; drain and set aside.

3 Using your fingertips or the heel of your hand, spread dough so it covers bottom of pan and comes ¾ of the way up the sides. Spread sauce over dough, then top with sausage mixture, and place pepperoni on top.

4 Bake 25 minutes, or until crust is crisp and brown. Sprinkle with cheese and cook 5 more minutes, or until cheese is melted. Cut into wedges and serve.

Test Kitchen Tip: If you don't have a springform pan, you can make this in an ovenproof deep skillet or a 10-inch cake pan.

Insider Info:

Last year, more than 1 million people applied to become contestants on Wheel of Fortune, yet fewer than 600 of them were selected. Turn to page xv to see how you can apply to get on the show. Also, keep an eye out to see if the Wheelmobile is coming to your part of the country, because when it does, you may be lucky enough to be called on stage, which could bring you one step closer to becoming a contestant. You can bet that when the Wheelmobile crew came to Chicago, it didn't take them long to find a winner—like this classic Chicago deep-dish pizza!

SUPER-EASY TACO HAND PIES

Makes 8 pies

½ pound ground beef

½ cup finely chopped onion

1 (1-ounce) package taco seasoning mix

1 teaspoon ground cumin

¼ teaspoon black pepper

1 cup black beans, rinsed and drained

1 cup frozen corn, thawed

1 (16.3-ounce) can refrigerated biscuits (8 biscuits)

½ cup shredded Cheddar cheese

1 egg

1 tablespoon water

1 Preheat oven to 375 degrees F.

2 In a large skillet over medium heat, cook ground beef and onion 5 to 6 minutes, or until browned, breaking up meat with a spoon; drain off liquid. Stir in taco seasoning, cumin, pepper, beans, and corn; heat 2 minutes, mixing well.

3 On a flat surface, using a rolling pin or a can, roll out each biscuit to about a 5-inch circle. Place about ⅓ cup beef mixture in center of each biscuit. Sprinkle each with a tablespoon of cheese and fold in half, forming a half moon shape. Seal edges with a fork, then place on baking sheet.

4 In a small bowl, beat egg and water. Brush entire top of each pie with egg wash. Bake 13 to 15 minutes, or until golden. Let cool slightly, then serve.

Serving Suggestion:

These are perfect on those nights when you want to eat dinner in front of the TV watching Wheel. Ya see, you can easily hold a hand pie in one hand while cheering on the contestants with the other. Oh, make sure you serve some fresh salsa with these for extra zing!

WINNING GREEN CHILE ENCHILADAS ®

Serves 8

- 1 (19-ounce) can green chile enchilada sauce
- 1 (10-½-ounce) can cream of chicken soup
- 1 (10-½-ounce) can cream of mushroom soup
- 2 (8.8-ounce) packages pre-cooked Spanish rice, heated according to package directions
- 1 (16-ounce) can refried beans
- 8 (6-inch) flour tortillas
- 1 cup shredded Monterey Jack cheese

1 Preheat oven to 350 degrees F. Coat a 9- x 13-inch baking dish with cooking spray.

2 In a large bowl, combine sauce and soups; mix well. Evenly spread 1 cup sauce mixture in prepared baking dish; set aside.

3 In another large bowl, mix rice and beans. Spoon an equal amount of mixture on center of each tortilla and roll up. Place seam side down in baking dish. Pour remaining sauce over tortillas.

4 Cover with aluminum foil and bake 35 minutes; remove from oven, sprinkle with cheese, and bake an additional 5 to 10 minutes, or until cheese is melted.

Test Kitchen Tip: If you want to make your own Spanish rice, you'll need about 4 cups. And you may want to finish these with fresh salsa or any of your favorite toppings.

Behind the Recipe:

"Every once in a while, we have a potluck lunch here at the studio. As soon as the sign-up list is posted, everyone asks me if I'll bring my enchiladas. I guess this means my work family loves these as much as my family at home."

Yvette Sapanza,
Assistant to the Executive Producer
12 years at WOF

TV SNACKIN' GLAZED MIXED NUTS

Makes 3 cups

2 egg whites

1 teaspoon vanilla extract

1 cup sugar

½ teaspoon salt

1 teaspoon cinnamon

1 pound pecan halves, walnuts, and almonds (about 3 cups)

1 Preheat oven to 250 degrees F. Coat a baking sheet with cooking spray.

2 In a large bowl, beat egg whites and vanilla until frothy. In another large bowl, combine sugar, salt, and cinnamon.

3 Add nuts to egg whites; stir to coat evenly. Remove half the nuts and toss them in the sugar mixture until well coated. Spread in a single layer on baking sheet. Repeat with remaining nuts.

4 Bake 1 hour, stirring every 15 minutes. Let cool, then store in an airtight container.

These are so good you might want to make a double batch. That way, you can share them, and you won't run out before it's time for the Bonus Round! These are also great to make as an edible gift. Just pack 'em in canning jars or decorative tins and you're good to go. Oh, don't forget a gift tag that says "From my kitchen to yours."

HOMEMADE DENVER BEER BREAD

Makes 1 loaf

3 cups self-rising flour

3 tablespoons sugar

1 (12-ounce) can beer, at room temperature

1 (4.5-ounce) can green chiles

3 tablespoons butter, melted

1 tablespoon chopped fresh parsley

½ teaspoon chili powder

1 Preheat oven to 350 degrees F. Coat an 8- x 4-inch loaf pan with cooking spray and dust with flour.

2 In a large bowl, combine flour and sugar. Gradually add beer, stirring just until dry ingredients are moistened. Stir in chiles. Spoon batter in pan.

3 Bake 55 to 60 minutes, or until toothpick inserted in center comes out clean. In a small bowl, mix butter, parsley, and chili powder; brush top of bread with mixture. Cool bread in pan 10 minutes; remove from pan and cool completely on a wire rack. Slice and serve.

Did You Know?

If you've never cooked with beer, then you're missing out. The Test Kitchen has slow roasted chicken with beer, braised ribs in it, and recently created a beer bread that was inspired by some amazing craft beers from Colorado, which has nearly 230 breweries. And although they didn't pioneer brewing, some say they just might have perfected it. When Vanna was in Denver, she stopped by Coors Field to get in the spirit of things.

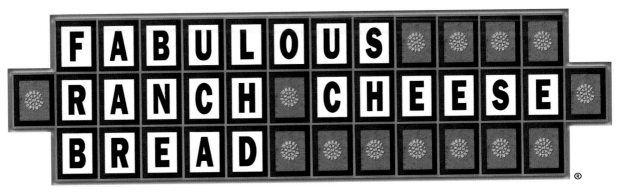

FABULOUS RANCH CHEESE BREAD ®

Serves 6

- 1 (8-ounce) package cream cheese, softened
- 2 tablespoons mayonnaise
- 1 (1-ounce) packet ranch mix
- 1 large loaf Italian bread
- 1 (8-ounce) package shredded four cheese mix

1 Preheat oven to 350 degrees F.

2 In a medium bowl, cream together cream cheese, mayonnaise, and ranch mix; set aside.

3 Slice bread lengthwise and place cut side up on baking sheet. Spread cream cheese mixture evenly over both sides. Sprinkle shredded cheese evenly over both sides.

4 Bake 10 to 15 minutes, or until bread is golden.

Test Kitchen Tip: Feel free to add some cooked bacon pieces over cheese before placing in the oven.

RECIPE CONTEST WINNER

"I've made this since my boys were little. Now they are in their late 20's and 30's. 'Til this day, whenever we have a meal at my house, I have to make this bread. We have it on all of the holidays and birthdays. Now, my grandchildren look forward to their dad making this for them. I make this whenever I go to a get-together with family and friends. It's always a fabulous hit!"

Shelly Frothingham
Owls Head, ME

NEW BABY BUGGY BANANA BREAD

Makes 1 loaf

½ stick butter, softened

1 cup sugar

2 eggs

3 ripe bananas, mashed

⅓ cup peanut butter (optional)

1-¼ cups flour

1 teaspoon baking soda

1-½ teaspoons vanilla extract

1 Preheat oven to 350 degrees F. Coat a 9- x 5-inch loaf pan with cooking spray.

2 In a large bowl, combine butter, sugar, and eggs until well blended. Add banana and peanut butter, if desired, beating until thoroughly mixed. Beat in flour, baking soda, and vanilla just until blended. Pour batter into loaf pan.

3 Bake 50 to 60 minutes, or until a toothpick inserted in center comes out clean. Let cool 10 minutes, then remove from pan.

Behind the Recipe:

This recipe came from Emil de Leon, a two-letter puzzle solver who's puzzle-solving skills went viral. He shared that he sometimes adds his own twist to his favorite super-moist banana bread. That twist is to stir in some peanut butter. He went on to say that, if you want, you could add in some chocolate chips, chopped nuts, or even berries.

Once this cools, you could cut it in half. That way, you can enjoy some now and freeze the rest for whenever you get the hankering for something truly homemade.

Once the Timer Started...

"I've been asked numerous questions regarding my experience on Wheel of Fortune, but the most unanimous request that I receive from Wheel Watchers is to share my experience in the Bonus Round. The whole experience was outstanding, but little did I know, the final 5 minutes of the show would change my entire life. I'd like to share what went on in my head, and even reveal some tips during those last 5 minutes—The Bonus Round.

"The category was "Thing." When the letters RSTLNE were given, the puzzle stood as NE_ * _ _ _ _ * _ _ _ _ _. When asked for my 3 consonants and a vowel, I called out HMDO, which are my go-to letters whenever I play the game at home. (Tip: It's good to have set letters that you're prepared to use before reaching the Bonus Round because you will always know what letters are and are not in the puzzle!)

"When Vanna White stood there motionless and shrugged, I knew that I had to work my puzzle-solving skills. The first word was obviously 'NEW.' I focused on the Used Letter Board and the puzzle, trying to fit in a 4-letter and a 5-letter-word. (Tip: On the show, a board is given with what letters have not been called yet, the Used Letter Board. Use that board to fill in the blanks of the puzzle!) With the letter 'B' as the first consonant on the Used Letter Board, I focused on words with that 'B' and found that 'BABY' was a possible word that fit. As for the 5-letter-word, using the word 'BABY, I thought of things that a baby could use or what could be found in a baby's room, eventually finding out that 'BABY BUGGY' was definitely a possibility, looking back at the letter 'B' again.

"Once the timer started, I yelled my first plausible solution, 'NEW BABY BUGGY,' thinking of other things that would fit, but luckily, I didn't have to think any further as the solution, 'NEW BABY BUGGY,' popped up on the puzzleboard. I received Pat Sajak's infamous pat-down, and he showed me the $45,000 prize. I was overjoyed with the whole experience and had no idea how viral this event would become . Thank you for reading!"

Emil de Leon, Two-Letter Puzzle Solver
Daly City, CA

EYE-OPENING SPICY BLOODY MARYS

Serves 6

1 (46-ounce) can tomato juice

3 tablespoons lime juice

1 tablespoon Worcestershire sauce

1 tablespoon prepared white horseradish, drained

1 teaspoon hot pepper sauce

½ teaspoon celery seed

¾ teaspoon salt

½ teaspoon black pepper

¾ cup vodka (optional)

6 celery stalks, trimmed and cleaned

Lime wedges (optional)

1 In a large covered jar or pitcher, combine tomato juice, lime juice, Worcestershire sauce, horseradish, hot pepper sauce, celery seed, salt, pepper, and vodka, if desired. Shake or mix until well blended.

2 Pour mixture over ice in tall glasses. Garnish with a celery stalk and lime wedge, if desired, and serve.

Fancy It Up:
To serve this like the restaurants do, rub the rim of the glass with a lime wedge then dip it into a saucer filled with kosher or sea salt, and you have a fancy schmancy-looking glass that is perfect for this eye-opening cocktail. These are a great way to round out brunch, maybe served with the Easy Breezy Brunch Soufflé on page 5, or the Baked Eggs Benedict Rolls on page 10.

PARTY PLEASIN' SANGRIA®

Serves 8

- 1 (6-ounce) container frozen limeade concentrate, thawed
- 1 (6-ounce) container frozen lemonade concentrate, thawed
- 1 (6-ounce) container frozen cranberry juice cocktail concentrate, thawed
- 4 cups dry red wine
- 2 cups cold water
- 1 lime, cut into chunks
- 1 orange, cut into chunks

1 In a large pitcher, combine limeade, lemonade, and cranberry juice concentrates; add wine and water and stir until well combined.

2 Stir in lime and orange chunks and serve immediately in ice-filled wine or tall glasses.

Serving Suggestion:

Serve this up with our Traditional All-in-One Paella on page 90. This is also great to serve during the heat of summer, since it's fruity and refreshing without packing too much of an alcoholic punch. And don't forget to nibble on the fruit when you're done sippin'... it's the best part!

FRANKIE & AVA'S DOGGIE TREATS

Makes 12 (3-inch) bones

- 1 cup all-purpose flour
- 1 cup whole wheat flour
- ½ cup wheat germ
- ½ cup nonfat dry milk
- 3 tablespoons vegetable shortening
- 1 teaspoon brown sugar
- ½ teaspoon salt
- 1 egg
- ½ cup water

1 Preheat oven to 350 degrees F. Coat a baking sheet with cooking spray.

2 In a large bowl, combine both flours, wheat germ, dry milk, shortening, brown sugar, and salt; mix until crumbly. Add egg and water; mix well.

3 On a lightly floured surface, knead dough until smooth. Using a rolling pin, roll out to ½-inch thickness. Using a dog bone-shaped cookie cutter or a knife, cut out biscuits and place on baking sheet.

4 Bake 25 to 30 minutes, or until golden. Remove to a wire rack to cool completely.

Behind the Recipe:

"Frankie and Ava are a pair of English Cocker Spaniel siblings. My mom and dad were Frankie and Ava's original human parents. They both loved Wheel of Fortune and were very proud that I worked for the show. My dad was an especially devoted viewer, and every night after dinner he would sit down on the couch with Frankie on one side and Ava on the other to watch and play along. In the last few years, first my mom and then my dad passed away. Frankie and Ava came to live with me and became part of my family. At this point, it's hard to imagine my life without them. They make me smile every day. And what better way to honor

my parents' memory and keep their traditions alive than to sit down on the couch after dinner with Frankie on one side and Ava on the other and watch our favorite game show. Frankie and Ava's favorite part of Wheel of Fortune? The "BONE-US ROUND" of course! There's probably only one thing they like more than Wheel of Fortune, and that would be ... TREATS!"

Lisa Dee
Producer
Marketing and Promotions
24 years at Wheel of Fortune

Did You Know? Although these are pet-friendly, before giving these to your dog, be sure he/she has no allergies to wheat, eggs, or dairy products. As always, it's a good idea to share this recipe with your vet just to make sure that it fits your dog's dietary regimen.

The Icing on the Cake!

"Being on Wheel of Fortune was one of the top highlights of my life! I'd started watching the show when I was about 4 years old, both the daytime and nighttime versions. From the time I started watching the show, Vanna White had already been a part of it and, at the ripe age of 4, I was hooked. I loved the show. And as my reading improved I tried to solve those puzzles as fast as I could. At the same time, I thought Vanna was the most gorgeous person ever, and I made it known enough that my entire family knew.

"Fast forward ~30 years and I am selected to actually appear on the show! My excitement level was off the charts as I thought, 'Maybe I'll get a chance to actually be in the same room as Vanna White.' On the morning of the taping, we were doing a walkthrough / rehearsal on stage, practicing spinning the wheel, when this woman in a ball cap and sweats comes on stage. Someone said, 'Ladies and gentlemen look who it is ... it's Vanna White!' I saw her and thought, 'That's it. I'm good. I can go home now.' But then, she approached all the contestants. She made her way closer to the Wheel and stepped up to address us, and she stepped up right next to me! She put her hand on my shoulder and wished us all good luck. This was a 30-year-old dream come true. And oh, by the way, she still looked as gorgeous as she did when I was 4.

"Everything that happened the rest of the day was a bonus as far as I'm concerned. A few hours later, before my show was about to be taped, I gave some details for Pat to use during the introductions. I decided to include my crush on Vanna White as a fun fact about me. When the show started taping, I solved the first Toss-Up so the introductions began with me. Pat mentioned hearing about a crush I had, so I mentioned my long crush on Vanna. I solved the 2nd Toss-Up with just one letter and Pat said he thought there was still a connection with Vanna and me. All in good fun, but man did I eat it up and love every second of it. I went on to solve every single main game puzzle and win what I was told was a record amount! So, not only did I get to meet Vanna White, I now have the highest total won in the main game in the history of the show!

"It can't get better, right? Wrong. After the bonus round, I had always been used to seeing Pat and Vanna chat for a few seconds on camera before signing off for the night. This time, they invited me to stand WITH them during the final segment, something I don't think is done very often at all. As my episode was the day after Christmas, Pat and Vanna mentioned having a Christmas present for me and Vanna said, 'I've been waiting 30 years for this,' and HUGGED ME...ON NATIONAL TELEVISION!" The cherry on top! The icing on the cake! It was such a great experience that I feel so fortunate to have had. If you ever have the chance to get a hug from Vanna White, I highly recommend it."

Matt DeSanto
Past Contestant

Million Dollar Desserts

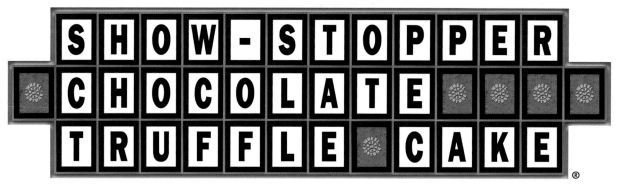

SHOW-STOPPER CHOCOLATE TRUFFLE CAKE

Serves 12

1 (16.5-ounce) package chocolate cake mix

1 (4-serving-size) package instant chocolate pudding mix

½ cup vegetable oil

3 eggs

1-¼ cups water

½ stick butter

1-½ cups semisweet chocolate chips, divided

¾ cup heavy cream, divided

3 cups confectioners' sugar

2 (14.1-ounce) cans dark chocolate rolled wafer cookies

1 Preheat oven to 350 degrees F. Coat 2 (9-inch) cake pans with cooking spray. In a large bowl, combine cake mix, pudding mix, oil, eggs, and water; mix well and divide evenly into pans. Bake 26 to 30 minutes, or until a toothpick inserted in center comes out clean. Cool slightly, then remove to a wire rack to cool completely.

2 In a microwaveable bowl, combine butter and 1 cup chocolate chips. Microwave 45 to 60 seconds, or until chocolate chips are melted, stirring occasionally until smooth. Stir in ½ cup heavy cream. Gradually add confectioners' sugar and beat with an electric mixer until smooth.

3 Place one cake layer on a platter and frost top. Place second layer on top of frosting and frost the sides only, not the top.

4 Place remaining chocolate chips in a small bowl. In a small saucepan, heat remaining heavy cream until hot, pour over chocolate chips, and stir until smooth and thickened. Pour on top of the cake and, with a spatula, frost only the top with this.

5 Arrange the cookies around the cake as shown. They will stick to the frosting. Tie a ribbon around the cake. Serve immediately or chill until ready to serve.

Insider Info:
Did you know that the Wheel gets its signature clicking sound from the 73 stainless steel pins that fly past three hard rubber flippers? Make sure you listen for that the next time you watch.

CHOCOLATE LOVER'S CHEESECAKE®

Serves 12

Ingredients

- 1 (14.3-ounce) package chocolate sandwich cookies, finely crushed
- ¾ stick butter, melted
- 4 (8-ounce) packages cream cheese, softened
- 1-¼ cups sugar
- 2 cups semisweet chocolate chips, melted
- 2 eggs
- ½ cup sour cream
- ¾ cup flour
- 1 teaspoon vanilla extract

1 Preheat oven to 350 degrees F. Coat the bottom of a 9-inch springform pan with cooking spray. In a medium bowl, mix crushed cookies and melted butter until well combined. Press into bottom and halfway up sides of pan. Chill until ready to use.

2 In a large bowl, beat cream cheese with sugar just until smooth. Beat in remaining ingredients until well combined. Spoon batter into crust.

3 Bake 55 to 60 minutes, or until firm. Remove from oven and let cool 2 to 3 hours at room temperature. Remove sides of springform pan; cover and chill at least 6 hours before serving.

Make it Fancy:

In a microwaveable bowl, melt 2 cups white baking chips with 1 tablespoon vegetable shortening on high power 1 to 2 minutes, stirring until smooth. Pour mixture into a wax paper-lined 9-inch springform pan bottom. Chill 30 minutes, or until set. Remove from pan and gently peel off wax paper. Place on a cutting board, and with a warm knife, carefully cut into 12 wedges. Arrange the wedges over the cheesecake as shown.

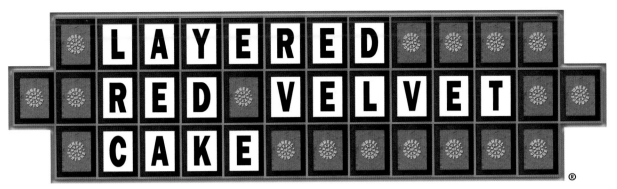

LAYERED RED VELVET CAKE

Serves 8

½ cup shortening

1-½ cups sugar

2 eggs

2 ounces red food coloring

2 tablespoons cocoa powder

1 cup buttermilk

2-½ cups flour

1 tablespoon vinegar

1 teaspoon vanilla extract

1 teaspoon baking soda

1 teaspoon salt

FROSTING

5 tablespoons flour

1 cup milk

1 cup sugar

2 sticks butter, softened

1 teaspoon vanilla extract

1 Preheat oven to 350 degrees F. Coat 2 (8-inch) cake pans with cooking spray and dust with flour.

2 In a large bowl with an electric mixer, cream shortening, 1-½ cups sugar, and eggs. In a small bowl, mix together food coloring and cocoa, making a paste. Beat into shortening mixture. Add ⅓ of the buttermilk and ⅓ of the flour at a time, alternating until well mixed. Add vinegar, vanilla, baking soda, and salt.

3 Divide evenly in pans. Bake 30 to 35 minutes, or until a toothpick inserted in center comes out clean. Cool slightly, then remove to a wire rack to cool completely.

4 Meanwhile, to make frosting, in a small saucepan over medium heat, whisk together flour and milk and cook until thickened, stirring constantly. Cool completely. In a large bowl, with an electric mixer, cream together sugar, butter, and remaining vanilla. Beat in flour mixture until fluffy; do not overmix. Refrigerate frosting 30 minutes, or until it has a stiff consistency. Place one cake layer on a platter and frost. Place second cake layer on top, and frost top and sides evenly. Refrigerate until ready to serve.

Behind the Recipe:

"Growing up, this was my favorite cake. My mom would make it for everyone's birthday per their request. Then, for someone's birthday, I baked the cake. From then on, everyone requested a red cake baked by Stevie for their birthday. I no longer live near my family, but every now and then, whenever I'm in town and it's someone's birthday, I'll bake the cake for old time's sake."

**Stevie Kloeber, Production Coordinator
4 years at Wheel of Fortune**

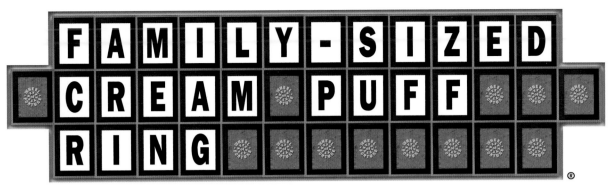

FAMILY-SIZED CREAM PUFF RING

Serves 12

1 cup water

1 stick butter, cut into quarters

¼ teaspoon salt

1 cup flour

4 eggs, at room temperature

1 (4-serving-size) package instant vanilla pudding mix

1 cup milk

1 (8-ounce) container frozen whipped topping, thawed

1 cup semi-sweet chocolate chips

½ cup heavy cream

1 Preheat oven to 400 degrees F.

2 In a medium saucepan over medium-high heat, bring water, butter, and salt to a boil. Add flour all at once and stir quickly with a wooden spoon until mixture forms a ball; remove from heat. Add 1 egg to mixture and beat with a wooden spoon to blend. Add remaining eggs, one at a time, beating well after each addition. Spoon dough into a resealable plastic bag and cut 1–1/2 inches off a corner. Pipe dough into an 8-inch circle on an ungreased 10-inch pizza pan, forming a ring. (It should look like a big donut.)

3 Bake 45 to 50 minutes, or until golden brown and puffy. Cool 15 minutes, then place on a serving platter to finish cooling.

4 Meanwhile, in a large bowl, whisk pudding and milk until thickened. Add whipped topping and mix until combined. Refrigerate 20 minutes to thicken. Using a serrated knife, cut ring in half horizontally, removing top. Evenly spoon vanilla pudding mixture onto bottom half of cream puff ring. Place top over pudding mixture.

5 Place chocolate chips in a medium bowl. In a small saucepan over medium-low heat, heat heavy cream just until hot. (Do not boil.) Pour over chocolate chips and stir constantly until smooth and thick. Spoon evenly over top of cream puff. Refrigerate until ready to serve.

GRANNY'S SOUR CREAM CAKE

Serves 10

3 sticks butter, softened, divided

3 cups granulated sugar

1 (8-ounce) container sour cream

6 eggs

3 cups flour

¼ teaspoon baking soda

2 teaspoons rum extract

1 (16-ounce) package confectioners' sugar

2 teaspoons almond extract

1 Preheat oven to 325 degrees F. Generously coat a tube pan with cooking spray and dust with flour.

2 In a large bowl with an electric mixer, cream together 2 sticks butter and the granulated sugar until light and fluffy. Blend in sour cream. Add eggs, one at a time, beating well after each addition. Combine flour and baking soda and gradually add to batter. Mix well, then add rum extract. Pour batter into pan.

3 Bake 1–¼ to 1–½ hours, or until a toothpick comes out clean. Cool 30 minutes, then turn out onto a serving plate. Let cool completely.

4 To make icing, in a large bowl, beat remaining butter, the confectioners' sugar, and almond extract until well blended. Spread evenly over cake.

Test Kitchen Tip: If you don't have a tube pan, you can make this in 2 (9- x 5-inch) loaf pans. Just bake 75 to 80 minutes, or until a toothpick comes out clean.

RECIPE CONTEST WINNER

"My grandmother was from Alabama and would make this cake when we went to visit her when I was a little girl. My grandmother loved to bake Southern-style desserts. So basically, the more sugar and butter the better. The smell of this cake baking brings back memories of those visits."

Susan Sweet-McMahan
Lecanto, FL

SMASHING PUMPKIN PIE CUPCAKES

Serves 16

16 gingersnap cookies

¾ cup flour

2 teaspoons pumpkin pie spice

¼ teaspoon baking soda

¼ teaspoon baking powder

¼ teaspoon salt

1 (15-ounce) can 100% pure pumpkin

¾ cup sugar

2 eggs

1 teaspoon vanilla extract

¾ cup evaporated milk

1-½ cups frozen whipped topping, thawed

Cinnamon for sprinkling

1 Preheat oven to 350 degrees F. Line 16 muffin cups with paper liners. Place a cookie in the bottom of each paper liner; set aside.

2 In a bowl, whisk together flour, pumpkin pie spice, baking soda, baking powder, and salt. In a large bowl, whisk together pumpkin, sugar, eggs, vanilla, and evaporated milk until well combined. Add in dry ingredients and whisk until well combined and batter is smooth. Fill each muffin cup about ¾ full.

3 Bake 25 to 30 minutes, or until set in center. Remove from oven and let cool 20 minutes. Remove cupcakes from pan and chill 30 minutes.

4 When ready to serve, top each cupcake with a dollop of whipped topping and sprinkle with cinnamon.

Behind the Scenes:

Almost every week on Wheel there's a new theme, and do you know what that means? A new look. Here, Shaun Page from the Art Department is decorating the set for Halloween. No bones about it, they do a great job! After a day of taping, that all comes down and it's on to the next theme.

STACKED SPIN-TACULAR PARTY CAKE ®

Serves 10

1 (16.5-ounce) package white cake mix, batter prepared according to package directions

1 cup rainbow sprinkles

6 cups confectioners' sugar

2 sticks butter, softened

½ cup vegetable shortening

3 tablespoons milk

1 teaspoon vanilla extract

1 (10.8-ounce) package mini candy-coated chocolates, separated by color

10 lollipop sticks (optional)

1 Preheat oven to 350 degrees F. Coat 2 (8-inch) cake pans with cooking spray. Stir sprinkles into prepared cake batter, then divide batter evenly between cake pans.

2 Bake 30 to 35 minutes, or until toothpick inserted in center comes out clean. Let cool 15 minutes, then remove cake from pans to wire rack to cool completely. Slice each cake in half horizontally to make 4 layers total.

3 In a large bowl, with an electric mixer, beat remaining ingredients except chocolates, 1 to 2 minutes, or until creamy.

4 Place 1 cake layer on platter and spread evenly with frosting. Repeat with remaining cake layers and frosting, finishing with top and sides of cake. Lightly score the top of the cake in 10 even wedges. Decorate each wedge with one color of candy-coated chocolates, alternating each wedge with a different color. (See photo.) Place lollipop sticks in each cake wedge, to resemble the spokes on the wheel, if desired. Serve, or refrigerate until ready to serve.

This frosting is so buttery-rich, it's really best served chilled right from the fridge. Trust us ... you won't be sorry when you try it!

PERFECTLY PEACHY CREAM PIE

Serves 8

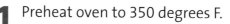

¾ cup flour

1 teaspoon baking powder

1 (4-serving-size) package cook & serve vanilla pudding mix

3 tablespoons butter, softened

1 egg

½ cup milk

1 (30-ounce) can sliced peaches, drained, with 3 tablespoons juice reserved

1 (8-ounce) package cream cheese, softened

½ cup plus 1 tablespoon sugar

½ teaspoon cinnamon

1 Preheat oven to 350 degrees F.

2 In a large bowl, combine flour, baking powder, pudding mix, butter, egg, and milk. Pour batter into 9-inch pie plate. Lay peaches on top.

3 Combine cream cheese, ½ cup sugar, and reserved peach juice. Drop this mixture in dollops over peaches and swirl around to spread over peaches.

4 In a small bowl, combine remaining sugar and the cinnamon; sprinkle over top of pie. Bake 30 to 35 minutes, or until a toothpick inserted in center comes out clean.

RECIPE CONTEST WINNER

"This was a favorite recipe that my mother taught me to make. My children love it and often ask me to make it as their birthday dessert. During peach season you can use fresh peaches that you peel and slice, and sometimes I'll also sprinkle a few fresh raspberries on top for an added treat."

Chris Jensen
Catonsville, MD

COUNTRY BERRY PATCH PIE®

Serves 6

Ingredients

- 1 egg
- 1 tablespoon water
- 1 (15-ounce) package refrigerated rolled pie crusts
- 2 cups quartered strawberries
- 1-¼ cups blueberries
- 1-¼ cups raspberries
- 1-¼ cups blackberries
- ¾ cup plus 1 tablespoon sugar
- ½ cup flour
- 1 tablespoon butter, melted

1 Preheat oven to 400 degrees F. In a small bowl, whisk egg and water; set aside.

2 Unroll 1 pie crust and place in a 9-inch pie plate, pressing crust firmly into pie plate. Place remaining pie crust on a work surface and using the plastic cap of a water bottle, cut 8 to 10 circles around edges, as shown below, leaving a 1-inch edge. Set aside cutouts.

3 In a large bowl, combine remaining ingredients except 1 tablespoon sugar; mix well then spoon into pie crust. Place top crust over berry mixture. Pinch together and trim edges to seal, then flute, if desired. Brush the egg wash over top of crust. Place cut-out pieces in a circle, overlapping, in the center of the pie; brush circles with egg wash. Sprinkle remaining sugar over crust.

4 Bake 40 to 45 minutes, or until crust is golden and filling is bubbly. Let cool before serving, or chill until ready to serve.

Did You Know?

This pie is perfect when summer berries are at their peak, but no worries, you can make this year-round by using frozen berries. After all, since frozen berries are frozen the same day they're picked, you can bet they'll taste just as fresh.

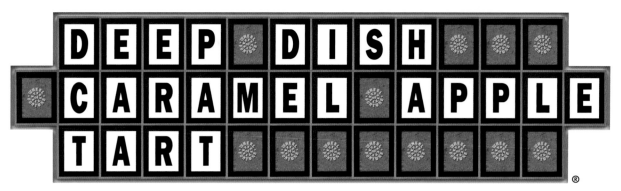

DEEP DISH CARAMEL APPLE TART®

Serves 8

- 1 (16.5-ounce) roll refrigerated sugar cookie dough, cut into 24 slices
- 4 large Granny Smith apples, peeled, cored, and thinly sliced
- ½ cup granulated sugar
- 1-½ teaspoons cinnamon
- 4 tablespoons flour, divided
- ½ cup packed brown sugar
- ½ cup old-fashioned oats
- 2 tablespoons butter
- ¼ cup caramel syrup

1. Preheat oven to 375 degrees F. Coat a 9-inch springform pan with cooking spray. Press cookie dough into bottom and halfway up sides of pan. Bake 10 minutes.

2. Meanwhile, in a large bowl, mix apples, granulated sugar, cinnamon, and 2 tablespoons flour. Toss to coat. Pour mixture evenly into crust.

3. In a small bowl, mix brown sugar, oats, remaining flour, and butter until crumbly. Sprinkle over apples.

4. Bake 40 to 45 minutes, or until crust is golden brown and apples are fork-tender. Cool 20 minutes, then remove side of pan. Cool at least 1 hour. When ready to serve, drizzle with caramel syrup.

Serving Suggestion:
How about serving this as part of your holiday dessert line-up, with a big scoop of vanilla ice cream or a dollop of freshly whipped cream?

It's probably a better idea than the way Vanna served her pie to Pat in a past show. I guess the good thing was there were no dishes or utensils to wash afterwards ... just Pat's suit!

DAD'S FAVORITE DESSERT

Serves 12

1 cup flour

1 stick butter

1 cup finely chopped pecans

1 (8-ounce) package cream cheese, softened

1 cup confectioners' sugar

1 (16-ounce) container frozen whipped topping, thawed, divided

1 (4-serving-size) package instant vanilla pudding

1 (4-serving-size) package instant chocolate pudding

3 cups cold milk

Grated chocolate for garnish

1 Preheat oven to 350 degrees F. Coat a 9- x 13-inch baking dish with cooking spray.

2 In a medium bowl, combine flour, butter, and pecans; mix well, then pat crust into baking dish. Bake 15 to 20 minutes, or until golden; let cool.

3 In a medium bowl, beat cream cheese and confectioners' sugar until smooth. Fold in ½ the whipped topping, then spread evenly over crust.

4 In a medium bowl, combine pudding mixes with milk and whisk until smooth and thickened. Spread evenly over cream cheese layer. Top with remaining whipped topping and garnish with grated chocolate. Cover and refrigerate at least 2 hours before serving.

Lighten It Up:
If you'd like, you can always use reduced fat cream cheese, a lighter whipped topping, and skim milk. The Test Kitchen tried it both ways, and although they both work just fine, the way the Corwin family serves it is unbelievably good!

It's a Family Affair

"My Mom, Robin, worked on the show many years ago where she met my Dad, Mark Corwin, when he was the Associate Director. They fell in love, got married, and had my brother and me. When I was a teen, my Mom retired so she could spend more time with us, doing all the stuff that Moms do. After we grew up, I started to work on the show as a Booth Production Assistant. My brother, Michael, became a Cameraman on Wheel, which meant we both got to work with our Dad. He was an Emmy award-winning Director of the show for over a decade, and it was truly an honor working with him. Unfortunately, he is no longer with us, but he left an impact on everyone he worked with and was loved by all.

"This recipe was one of his favorites. We still make it today as just one way to pay homage to the World's Greatest Dad."

Chloe Corwin, Booth Production Assistant
9 years at Wheel of Fortune

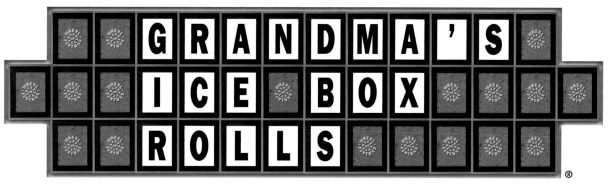

GRANDMA'S ICE BOX ROLLS

Makes 2 dozen rolls

5 cups flour, divided, plus extra for sprinkling

2 tablespoons plus ¼ cup sugar, divided

½ pound shortening

3 eggs

1-¼ cups whole milk, divided

1 (¼-ounce) packet yeast (dissolved in ¼ cup warm water)

2 cups walnuts, finely chopped

½ cup golden raisins

1 In a large bowl, combine 4 cups flour, 2 tablespoons sugar, the shortening, eggs, 1 cup milk, and the yeast, mixing until a dough forms. Knead dough but do not overwork; sprinkle with flour, cover, and refrigerate overnight.

2 In a medium bowl, mix walnuts, raisins, the remaining sugar, and the remaining milk; blend until a spreadable consistency is reached.

3 Preheat oven to 375 degrees F. Line a baking sheet with parchment paper.

4 Generously sprinkle a work surface with the remaining 1 cup flour. Divide dough into 2 pieces. Roll out first piece into a circle about ¼-inch thick; evenly spread ½ of nut mixture over circle. Cut into 12 triangles, then roll up like crescent rolls. Place on baking sheet. Repeat with second piece of dough. Bake 25 minutes, or until golden.

Behind the Recipe:

"My grandmother was from Czechoslovakia and lived to cook for her family. This recipe was put together by watching our grandmother make these, then collaborating with all the other grandkids to make sure we had it right. She was very protective of her recipes and, most of the time, if you asked her for one, she would purposely leave something out just so that you would have to come back to her to get the 'real' taste."

Jody Vaclav,
Assistant Art Director/Set Designer
13 years at Wheel of Fortune

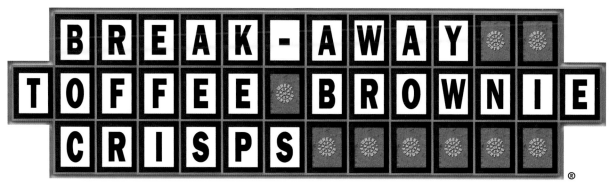

BREAK-AWAY TOFFEE BROWNIE CRISPS

Makes 12 to 15 pieces

2 large egg whites

½ cup sugar

2 tablespoons cocoa powder

¼ cup vegetable oil

½ teaspoon vanilla extract

¼ teaspoon salt

¼ teaspoon baking powder

1 tablespoon nonfat dry milk powder

½ cup all-purpose flour

¼ cup toffee bits

¼ cup mini chocolate chips

1 Preheat oven to 325 degrees F. Line a rimmed baking sheet with aluminum foil.

2 In a large bowl, with a whisk, beat egg whites until foamy. Gradually whisk in sugar, then the cocoa powder, oil, and vanilla until smooth. Slowly whisk in the salt, baking powder, and nonfat dry milk powder. Add flour and continue whisking until smooth.

3 Pour batter onto prepared baking sheet and spread as thinly as possible using the back of a spoon or spreader. Evenly sprinkle with toffee bits and chocolate chips.

4 Bake on center rack 20 minutes; remove from oven. With a pizza cutter or knife, cut into uneven pieces (see photo) without separating. Return to oven 5 minutes. Remove from oven and let cool completely. Break apart and serve, or store in an airtight container until ready to serve.

Test Kitchen, Mr. Food Hints & Tips

These are perfect for gift-giving. Pack them in a decorative tin, top it off with a ribbon, and make sure you include a copy of the recipe because these are so good, they're gonna ask you for it after one bite!

WHEEL OF FORTUNE COOKIES ®

Makes 20 cookies

3 egg whites

¾ cup sugar

1 stick butter, melted

½ teaspoon vanilla extract

2 tablespoons water

1 cup flour

20 fortunes, written on ½-inch x 2-inch strips of paper

1 Preheat oven to 375 degrees F. Coat 2 baking sheets with cooking spray.

2 In a large bowl, with an electric mixer, beat egg whites and sugar until frothy, but not stiff. Add butter, vanilla, water, and flour and beat on low until well combined.

3 Place a tablespoon of batter on baking sheet, making a 2–½-inch circle. Make only 2 more circles with batter, since you will need to fold these quickly as soon as they come out of the oven, before they cool. Once they cool they cannot be shaped.

4 Bake 5 to 7 minutes, or until edges turn golden. (Center will stay pale in color.) Quickly remove cookies with spatula and place upside down on cutting board. Place a fortune message in center of cookie, then gently fold cookie in half. Bring the two points together creating a horseshoe shape. Place folded cookies into the cups of a muffin tin to hold their shape until firm. Repeat with remaining batter. When all cookies are in muffin cups, return to oven 10 minutes to crisp up. Let cool.

Did You Know?
There are 46 puzzle categories. How many can you name? This recipe title would be the perfect example of when Pat would say, "The category for the puzzle is 'Before and After.'"

"OOH IT'S SO GOOD!!"

SURPRISE POTATO CHIP COOKIES

Makes 50 cookies

4 sticks unsalted butter, softened

1 cup sugar

2 teaspoons vanilla extract

3-½ cups flour

1 cup crushed plain potato chips

1 cup finely chopped nuts

1 Preheat oven to 350 degrees F.

2 In a large bowl, cream together butter, sugar, and vanilla until smooth. Mix in flour, potato chips, and nuts until well combined. Drop by teaspoonfuls onto baking sheets.

3 Bake 10 to 15 minutes, or to desired crispness.

Test Kitchen Tip: Feel free to cut this recipe in half. You can add a little more potato chips if you like, and any nuts will work here – whatever you like!

Behind the Recipe:

"My grandmother would make these, and they were always a hit. When people ask what kind of cookie it is, we get the greatest reactions. I love introducing these to friends. How can you go wrong with butter, vanilla, sugar, nuts, and salty potato chips?"

**Christy Myers, Travel Coordinator
14 years at Wheel of Fortune**

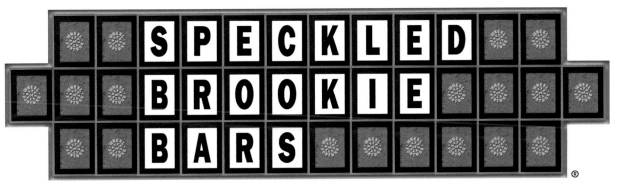

SPECKLED BROOKIE BARS

Makes 24 bars

- 2 (19.8-ounce) boxes brownie mix, batter prepared according to package directions
- 1 (16.5-ounce) roll refrigerated chocolate chip cookie dough, cut into ¼-inch-thick slices
- ½ cup chopped walnuts
- ½ cup chocolate chips

1 Preheat oven to 350 degrees F. Coat 9- x 13-inch baking dish with cooking spray.

2 Pour half the brownie batter into the baking dish and spread evenly. Place cookie dough slices over brownie batter. Pour remaining brownie batter over top of cookie dough slices. Sprinkle with nuts and chocolate chips.

3 Bake 45 to 50 minutes, or until a toothpick inserted in the center comes out clean. Let cool, then cut into bars.

Serving Suggestion: These are great to make on the weekend. After they cool, cut them into bars, wrap each one in plastic wrap, and store them in the freezer. When you get a hankerin' for something decadently good right before Wheel comes on, unwrap one (or two), pop them in the microwave for a few seconds and you're good to go.

Did You Know?

*If you are thinking, "What the heck is a brookie?" just read on. It's a baked dessert that is part **br**ownie and part **c**ookie. It's perfect for when your family can't decide between the two. And the nice thing about this is, you can always switch up the flavor of cookie dough if you want. Maybe sugar cookie dough one time, chocolate chip cookie dough another time...you get the idea.*

SPINNING SUGAR PINWHEELS

Makes 24 cookies

1-½ sticks butter, softened

1 cup sugar

1 egg

1 teaspoon vanilla extract

⅛ teaspoon salt

2 cups flour

9 drops red food color

½ cup colored sugar crystals

1 In a large bowl with an electric mixer on medium speed, beat together butter and sugar. Add egg, vanilla, and salt; beat until smooth. Stir in flour and knead lightly until a soft dough forms. Divide dough in half. Place 1 piece of the dough in a bowl and, wearing gloves, add food color and knead until evenly mixed. Wrap each piece in plastic wrap and chill about 1 hour.

2 On a floured surface, roll out each piece of dough separately to form a rectangle about ¼-inch thick. Brush the red dough with a little water, then place the plain dough over it. Trim edges. Gently start rolling, jelly roll-style, starting with a wide end and brushing lightly with water as you go along. Wrap in plastic wrap and chill 1 hour, or until firm.

3 Preheat oven to 350 degrees F. Coat baking sheets with cooking spray. In a shallow dish, place colored sugar crystals. Cut dough into ¼-inch slices and roll outer edges in sugar. Place on baking sheets. Sprinkle with more sugar crystals. Bake 10 to 12 minutes, or until light golden. Remove from baking sheets and place on wire rack to cool.

If you're having a Wheel-watching party, maybe make a few batches and make each one a different color. That'll give you one colorful cookie platter for sure! It'll be one that'll have everyone asking, "Where did ya get these cookies? They look wheely good!" There's no need to let anyone know how easy these are.

MY MOM'S CHOCOLATE CHIP COOKIES®

Makes 3 dozen cookies

2 sticks butter, softened

¼ cup granulated sugar

¾ cup brown sugar

2 eggs

1 teaspoon vanilla extract

2-¼ cups flour

1 teaspoon baking soda

1 (3.9-ounce) package instant vanilla pudding mix

1 (12-ounce) package chocolate chips

1 Preheat oven to 375 degrees F.

2 In a large bowl with an electric mixer, combine butter, granulated sugar, and brown sugar; beat until creamy. Beat in eggs and vanilla. Slowly add flour, baking soda, and pudding mix; mix until well combined. Stir in chocolate chips.

3 Drop mixture by rounded teaspoonfuls onto baking sheets.

4 Bake 8 to 10 minutes, or until golden. Cool 2 minutes, then remove cookies to a wire rack to cool completely.

RECIPE CONTEST WINNER

"Mom bakes these cookies every holiday. Everyone loves them and raves about them. She gives a batch of cookies, as a gift, to those people who have helped her throughout the year. I live in Florida (Mom lives in Indiana), and I request a batch of her cookies for the road trip home each year. Nobody makes them better than Mom. Try them for yourself."

Cindy Burns
Crystal River, FL

WRAPPED CANDY PRESENTS®

Makes 24 cookies

1 stick butter, softened

¾ cup confectioners' sugar

1 tablespoon vanilla extract

1-½ cups flour

⅛ teaspoon salt

24 chocolate candy kisses

½ cup white chocolate chips

Red and green decorating sugar for garnish

1 Preheat oven to 350 degrees F.

2 In a large bowl with an electric mixer, beat butter, confectioners' sugar, and vanilla. Add flour and salt, and mix until a soft dough forms. (If dough is dry, add 1 tablespoon milk.) Wrap a tablespoon of dough around each chocolate candy and place on a baking sheet.

3 Bake 12 to 15 minutes, or until light brown on bottom. Cool 15 to 20 minutes.

4 Place white chocolate chips in in a microwaveable bowl and microwave 60 seconds; stir until smooth. Dip top of each cookie in white chocolate and sprinkle immediately with red and green sugar. Let cool.

Insider Info:

When the Mr. Food Test Kitchen team first visited with the folks at Wheel of Fortune, they were invited to watch the taping of a show. It may have been mid-September outside the studio, but inside it looked more like Christmas. You see, they tape the shows months before they actually air since they need to be edited and distributed to your local TV station. These cookies, which happen to be one of the Test Kitchen's most popular holiday recipes, are a holiday gift to you in tribute to that very first visit.

NO-PASSPORT-REQUIRED BAKLAVA ®

Makes 24 pieces

3 cups chopped walnuts

¼ cup sugar

1 teaspoon cinnamon

1-½ sticks butter, melted, divided

½ of (16-ounce) package frozen phyllo dough, thawed

SYRUP

½ stick butter

¾ cup honey

¾ cup sugar

¾ cup water

1 teaspoon vanilla extract

1 Preheat oven to 350 degrees F. In a medium bowl, combine walnuts, sugar, and cinnamon; set aside. Brush a thin layer of melted butter over the bottom of a 9- x 13-inch baking dish.

2 Unroll the phyllo sheets onto a flat work surface. Remove one sheet of phyllo dough and place it on the bottom of the baking dish, trimming if necessary to fit. Brush lightly with butter. Repeat with 6 more sheets, then sprinkle half the nut mixture over the phyllo. Place a sheet of phyllo on top of nuts, and lightly brush with butter. Repeat 4 more times. Sprinkle the remaining nut mixture on the phyllo, then layer with 7 more sheets of phyllo, brushing each with butter.

3 Using a sharp knife, cut the unbaked baklava on the diagonal in a diamond pattern before baking 40 to 45 minutes, or until golden brown.

4 In a medium saucepan over medium heat, combine syrup ingredients. Bring to a boil, then reduce heat to low. Simmer 5 minutes, stirring constantly. Pour evenly over the baklava. Let sit 2 to 4 hours, or until completely cooled, before serving.

Test Kitchen Tip: Remember to keep the phyllo sheets covered with a damp paper towel to prevent them from drying out while working with them.

This recipe was created for a recent Fabulous Food week, when the prize was a trip to Turkey. But the good thing about this international favorite is, although many countries claim its origin, we can enjoy it without a passport.

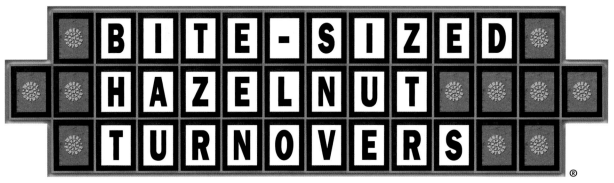

BITE-SIZED HAZELNUT TURNOVERS

Makes 24 turnovers

2 sticks butter, softened

1 (8-ounce) package cream cheese, softened

2-1/2 cups flour

1/2 teaspoon salt

1 cup chocolate hazelnut spread

1 egg, lightly beaten

1/3 cup finely chopped hazelnuts

Confectioners' sugar for sprinkling

1 In a large bowl with an electric mixer, cream together butter and cream cheese until light and fluffy. Gradually add flour and salt to mixture until combined.

2 Divide dough into 4 equal parts, wrap each with plastic wrap, and refrigerate at least 1 hour. Preheat oven to 350 degrees F. Line baking sheet with parchment paper.

3 On a floured surface, roll out one piece of dough to a 9- x 6-inch rectangle. Cut dough into 6 (3-inch) squares. Place a heaping teaspoon of chocolate hazelnut spread in center of each square. Moisten edges of dough with water, fold over diagonally, and seal using a fork. Place on prepared baking sheet. Brush with egg and sprinkle with nuts.

4 Bake 15 to 20 minutes, or until lightly golden. Let cool slightly, then sprinkle with confectioners' sugar.

Share Your Thoughts:

The best thing about these is that they blend a classic from-scratch cream cheese dough with a very trendy hazelnut chocolate filling. The results are...well, the results aren't all in until you weigh in with your thoughts. And the best way to do that is to post your comments on the Mr. Food Test Kitchen Facebook page. Just go to Facebook and then type in "Mr. Food Test Kitchen" to find it.

BACKSTAGE CRISPY SWIRLS

Serves 15

½ stick butter

1 (10.5-ounce) package mini marshmallows

5 cups crispy rice cereal

1 cup peanut butter

¾ cup semi-sweet chocolate chips

1 Preheat oven to 200 degrees F. Line a 10- x 15-inch rimmed baking sheet with wax paper and generously coat wax paper with cooking spray.

2 In a large saucepan over low heat, melt butter. Add marshmallows and stir until completely melted. Remove from heat and stir in rice cereal until evenly coated.

3 Press mixture evenly into baking sheet. Spread peanut butter evenly over top. Evenly sprinkle chocolate chips over peanut butter. Place in oven 2 minutes. Remove from oven and spread chocolate evenly. Let cool 10 minutes.

4 Roll up jellyroll-style, starting with the long side, peeling away the wax paper as you roll. Place seam-side down on baking sheet and refrigerate 30 to 45 minutes, or until chocolate has set. Cut into slices and serve.

If you'd like to precut these so they are ready to grab 'n' go, make sure you wrap them in wax paper, not plastic wrap, or you'll end up with a sticky mess. And if Vanna plans on eating these backstage, she better wash her hands before revealing any letters, or her fingers might just stick to the puzzleboard.

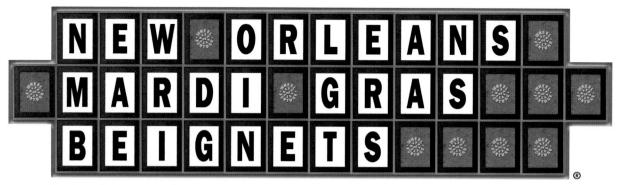

NEW ORLEANS MARDI GRAS BEIGNETS

Makes 3-½ dozen beignets

- 1 (1-pound) loaf frozen bread dough, thawed
- ¼ cup plus 1 tablespoon confectioners' sugar, divided
- 2 cups vegetable shortening

1 Place dough in a medium bowl and dust with 1 tablespoon confectioners' sugar. Using your hands, knead sugar into dough. Lightly dust a cutting board and rolling pin with flour. Roll out dough to an 8-inch by 20-inch rectangle. Cut into 2-inch squares.

2 In a large deep skillet over medium heat, heat shortening until hot, but not smoking. Add dough squares a few at a time and cook in batches about 30 seconds per side, or until golden. Drain on a paper towel-lined platter.

3 Sprinkle beignets with remaining confectioners' sugar and serve warm.

Did You Know?

Beignets were first introduced to New Orleans in the 18th century from French colonists. As the locals discovered this new treasure, beignets quickly became an important part of Creole cooking. They were so popular that in 1986 they were declared the official donut of the state of Louisiana. How's that for some fun facts to share when you serve these to your family?

CELEBRATING New Orleans

Over the years, Wheel of Fortune has saluted the great city and people of New Orleans many times. It's hard not to fall in love with this city—and its food. If you go, make sure you try the beignets (fried dough) covered in confectioners' sugar. Until then, here is an easy version of them that you can make at home. Warning: when you eat 'em, they can get pretty messy, as you can see!

COFFEE PECAN BALLS

Makes 96 balls

2 sticks unsalted butter, softened

2-½ cups confectioners' sugar, divided

2 teaspoons vanilla extract

2 cups flour

2 cups finely chopped pecans

1 tablespoon instant coffee

1 In a large bowl, cream butter. Beat in ½ cup confectioners' sugar and the vanilla. Add flour and pecans, blending well. Chill at least 2 hours or overnight.

2 Preheat oven to 350 degrees F. Cut dough into 4 pieces. Return to refrigerator so dough stays chilled. Working with 1 piece of dough at a time, place on work surface and cut in half. Roll each piece into a log and cut each log into approximately 12 equal parts. Shape each into a ball; place on baking sheets. Repeat until all dough is used.

3 Bake 15 minutes, or until lightly browned.

4 Place remaining confectioners' sugar in a shallow dish. While cookies are still warm, place a few at a time in the confectioners' sugar, tossing gently to coat well. Cool on racks.

5 Combine instant coffee with leftover confectioners' sugar in shallow dish. Roll cooled cookies again to coat well.

Behind the Recipe:

"My Great Aunt Pauline baked these cookies for me when I was a little girl. One time she gave some of these cookies to a friend. He told her, 'When I ate them, I felt like I had died and gone to heaven.' My Great Aunt Pauline is 92 years old, was a WAVE in World War II, won ribbons for her cookie recipes at county fairs, and continues to bake cookies for family and friends."

Renee Hoss-Johnson,
Production Designer
30 years at Wheel of Fortune

WHEEL WATCHIN' SNACK MIX®

Makes 12 cups

- 4 cups honey graham cracker cereal
- 2 cups coarsely crushed pretzels
- 6 cups popped popcorn
- 12 ounces chocolate almond bark
- 1 cup toffee bits

1 Line 2 rimmed baking sheets with wax paper. In a large bowl, stir together the cereal, pretzels, and popcorn.

2 Melt the almond bark according to package directions. Pour over cereal mixture and stir until evenly coated.

3 Pour mixture onto baking sheets, evenly sprinkle with toffee bits, and let cool completely. Break into chunks and store in a tightly sealed container.

Test Kitchen, Mr. Food Hints & Tips

If you're not familiar with chocolate almond bark, it can be found in the supermarket alongside all the other baking stuff. Make sure you look next to the chocolate chips; it's probably there. And if you're thinking that almond bark is loaded with almonds, although that would make sense, it's simply chocolate that's designed to be easily melted.

DECADENT CARAMEL-NOUGAT CANDY BARS

Makes 16 bars

- 2 cups semi-sweet chocolate chips, divided
- 2 teaspoons vegetable shortening, divided
- 1 (7-ounce) jar marshmallow crème
- 1 teaspoon vanilla extract
- 1-½ cups confectioners' sugar
- 2 tablespoons creamy peanut butter
- 1 cup unsalted peanuts
- 1 (11-ounce) package caramels
- ¼ cup heavy cream

1 Line the bottom of an 8-inch square baking dish with parchment or wax paper.

2 In a small saucepan over low heat, melt 1 cup chocolate chips and 1 teaspoon shortening, stirring until smooth. Pour mixture into baking dish and spread evenly. Place in freezer 5 minutes, or until hardened.

3 In a large bowl, combine marshmallow crème, vanilla, confectioners' sugar, and peanut butter. Using a wooden spoon, mix until a soft dough forms. Press dough evenly over chocolate layer. Sprinkle peanuts on top, gently pressing into dough.

4 In a small saucepan over medium heat, combine caramels and heavy cream; cook until melted, stirring constantly. Evenly pour over peanuts, spreading quickly before it hardens. Refrigerate 5 minutes, or until set.

5 Melt remaining chocolate chips and remaining teaspoon of shortening until smooth, and evenly pour on top. Refrigerate 30 minutes, or until set. Using a sharp knife, cut into 2-inch bars. Cover and refrigerate any leftovers.

Warning...*these are very addictive and have been known to cause uncontrollable smiles, giggles, and the desire to hide them from your friends. Actual results may vary. When you're watching Wheel, you may want to wait and eat these after the Bonus Round, since all the excitement at one time could be too much.*

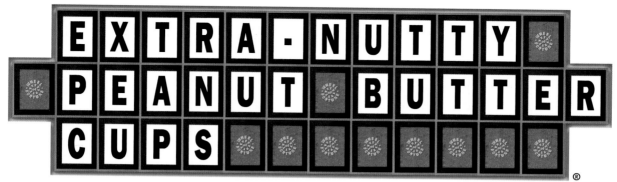

EXTRA-NUTTY PEANUT BUTTER CUPS®

Makes 12 cups

1 (11.5-ounce) package milk chocolate chips, divided

3 tablespoons vegetable shortening, divided

1-½ cups confectioners' sugar

1 cup crunchy peanut butter

½ stick butter, softened

⅓ cup coarsely chopped peanuts

1 Line a 12-cup muffin tin with paper liners.

2 In a small saucepan over low heat, melt 1–1/4 cups chocolate chips and 2 tablespoons shortening, stirring just until mixture is smooth. Allow to cool slightly; mixture should still be pourable.

3 Starting halfway up each paper liner, spoon about 2 teaspoons chocolate mixture over inside of liners, completely covering bottom half of each liner. Chill about 30 minutes, or until firm.

4 In a large bowl, combine confectioners' sugar, peanut butter, and butter; mix well. (Mixture will be dry.) Spoon evenly into chocolate cups and press filling down firmly.

5 Place remaining chocolate chips and remaining shortening in saucepan and melt over low heat, stirring just until mixture is smooth. Spoon equal amounts into cups, spreading to completely cover peanut butter mixture. Sprinkle with chopped peanuts. Cover and chill at least 2 hours, or until firm.

Test Kitchen Hints & Tips — Mr. Food

These homemade, nutty, peanut butter cups are perfect for nibbling on while watching Wheel. Maybe cut 'em into wedges; this way you can pace yourself from the first Toss-Up Round right through the part when Pat and Vanna chit-chat about...whatever. If they'd try these, the only thing they'd be talking about after the Bonus Round is how much better these are than the store-bought ones.

MOM'S EASY CHERRY COBBLER

Serves 6

- 1 (21-ounce) can cherry pie filling
- 1 (16.5-ounce) package yellow cake mix
- 1 stick butter, melted
- 3 tablespoons lemon juice
- ½ cup flaked coconut
- ¼ cup sliced almonds

1 Preheat oven to 325 degrees F. Coat an 8-inch square baking dish with cooking spray.

2 Place pie filling in baking dish, spreading evenly. Sprinkle with cake mix, then drizzle with butter. Drizzle lemon juice over top, then sprinkle with coconut and almonds.

3 Bake 55 minutes, or until top is golden.

Test Kitchen Tip: Looking to make this vegan? Feel free to substitute a vegan buttery spread for the butter. That's what Ken does, to honor his mom.

Behind the Recipe:

"This was my Mom's recipe and is one of my favorite desserts. I love it. It's very simple and very tasty. My dad loved cherries, so Mom made it with cherry pie filling, but you can substitute apple or peach pie filling if you'd like. Whenever I make this, it reminds me of my folks. Hope you enjoy!"

Ken Weiner
Segment Producer
7 years at Wheel of Fortune

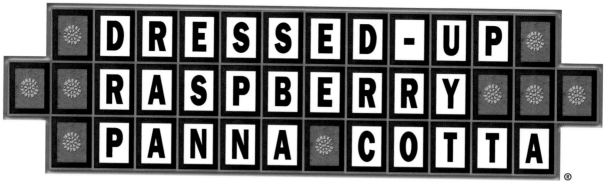

DRESSED-UP RASPBERRY PANNA COTTA ®

Serves 6

- 1 envelope unflavored gelatin
- ½ cup milk
- 2-½ cups heavy cream
- 1 cup sugar, divided
- 2 teaspoons vanilla extract
- 1 cup frozen raspberries

1 In a small bowl, sprinkle gelatin over milk; let stand about 5 minutes, or until gelatin is softened.

2 Meanwhile, in a large saucepan, combine heavy cream, ½ cup sugar, and the vanilla. Over medium-low heat, simmer until sugar has dissolved, stirring occasionally. (Do not let it boil.) Remove saucepan from heat, add gelatin mixture, and stir to completely dissolve gelatin.

3 Pour hot mixture through a fine mesh strainer into a large glass bowl, then carefully pour or spoon into custard cups. Refrigerate at least 6 hours or overnight.

4 Meanwhile, in a small saucepan over medium-high heat, combine raspberries and remaining sugar; bring to a boil, stirring occasionally. Reduce heat to low and simmer 5 to 6 minutes, or until berries have broken apart and sugar has dissolved. Let cool, then refrigerate until ready to use. Top each serving with raspberry sauce.

Behind the Recipe:

As you can imagine, since Wheel tapes many shows back-to-back in one day, Vanna has to quickly change her wardrobe between each one, which means she needs a bit of help. That's where Kathi Nishimoto, Vanna's Wardrobe Key Costumer for the last 33 seasons comes in. She ensures that Vanna looks just right. Vanna said that Kathi often brings in a homemade dessert to share with her and the team on tape days. She specifically mentioned that her Panna cotta was amazing. So, Kathi, thank you for sharing that inspiration ... and for making sure Vanna always looks her best.

VANNA BANANA PUDDING®

Serves 8

½ cup sugar, divided

⅔ cup flour

⅛ teaspoon salt

6 eggs, separated

4 cups milk

1 teaspoon vanilla extract

1 (11-ounce) box vanilla wafer cookies

3 ripe bananas, sliced

1 Preheat oven to 350 degrees F. In a large saucepan, combine ¼ cup sugar, the flour, and salt. Whisk in egg yolks and heat over medium heat until a paste is formed, stirring constantly. Reduce heat to low. Slowly whisk in milk until smooth. Cook about 10 minutes, or until thickened, whisking continuously. Remove from heat and stir in vanilla.

2 Spread a small amount of the custard on the bottom of a 2 quart casserole dish; cover with a layer of cookies, then top with a layer of sliced bananas. Spoon ⅓ of the remaining custard over bananas and continue with layers, ending with custard.

3 In a large bowl with an electric mixer, beat egg whites, gradually adding remaining sugar, until soft peaks form. Spoon over top layer, spreading it evenly until the entire surface is covered and the edges are sealed.

4 Bake 10 to 15 minutes, or until the meringue is golden. Serve warm or refrigerate until ready to serve.

Behind the Recipe:

"Growing up in the South, banana pudding was my family's go-to dessert, and no one made it like my mom. I still remember, as a little girl I'd watch her make this, and when she wasn't looking I would sneak a taste. Boy, was I quick! Today, I still make this the same way my mom did all those years ago when I'm craving a hug from my mom and some good old Southern comfort."

Vanna White, Co-Host
32 years at Wheel of Fortune

Index
Recipes in Alphabetical Order

Did you guess right? Answers from page 118: *E, B, C, D, A*